Foreword

This letter to Eugene, the young man who murdered my daughter, tries to convey the story of how I have searched for an ideal and how I've struggled to do that. I never imagined being challenged with such a painful and terrible reality of life.

I made a commitment to myself and God to live a true life. I needed to share Jin Joo's life with Eugene and some of my life stories.

Our children are precious because they are the future. How can we impart our hope that they will inherit the ideal of goodness and beauty in their lives and care about others in the human family?

God gave us life and freedom, but is it for us alone?

These stories also tell about the incredible life of Father and Mother Moon and the unwavering dedication of many of my brothers and sisters in the movement who have given a life of service to God and the world. I hope my story can reflect the lives of those who have given so much and have been misunderstood, quickly relegated to the impression of being crazy or brainwashed by their families, friends and media.

Jin Joo Ellen Byrne

Dear Eugene,

As you know, it has been twenty-two years since we lost our first child, Jin Joo. You were the last person who saw her alive. It is not only our family that still grieves for her but a whole community that knew her and loved her. As grieving parents, our hearts go out to all those who have lost their loved ones, especially parents who lost their children. I have thought long and hard, wondering how to convey to you the emotions of a father, a parent and a man striving for holiness in my lifetime. How does a man deal with and treat someone who has murdered his daughter and abused her most terribly?

It came to me as a message from heaven that I should write you a letter. The title "Dear Eugene" blasted into my mind as I stepped into my shower one cold morning and gave me the courage to write this story to you. It is also for those who seek after goodness and purity, who have a desire to live an extraordinary life, a happy life and, ultimately, see a world harmony and peace.

After I wrote down the thoughts I could include, this account began to develop so you could understand our lives and realize how precious our murdered daughter, Jin Joo Ellen, was to us. I am certainly not the most eloquent writer, but I hope to express my honesty through this letter, which has become my memoir.

The stories I wrote reminded me that I have seen glimpses of God working in my life.

My writing has been a continuous struggle because it is so painful to express my emotions. Nearly immediately after Jin Joo Ellen's death, I became absorbed in writing to you. The process of putting thoughts into words helped me to heal in some ways. I regret and am genuinely sorry that I must have neglected my wife and three other children's feelings when they needed me the most.

Deciding how to convey my story and all I had learned through my journey was challenging. The question about God's existence, the meaning and purpose of life here on this earth and after we die, love, truth, ideal and true goodness has been a constant quest in my life.

I needed a deeper understanding of God and the principles that govern our universe. I have always felt that a new truth must be revealed for the world to change because unbelievable sorrow flows through the ages of time. There appears to be no end to the madness we read about daily.

Somehow, humanity has been unable to solve the problems that have caused this chaos and confusion. It has become very sick, yet doesn't understand how mortally wounded it is.

I hope my writings can influence you to ponder your life.

This is a story of my search for truth and how I have struggled to reflect the heart of God and have a meaningful life.

Fortunately, I found a model to show me how to achieve that.

Innovators and trendsetters usually are only accepted once their ideas filter into society.

I have always regretted not asking my Irish and Scottish grandparents about their lives, so this letter will also explain my life journey to my dear wife of more than forty years, Izabela, our three children and their descendants.

Our Daughter is Missing

On August 28th 2002, my wife had just come home with our son when the telephone rang. It was a little after 3:00 p.m. in Seattle.

Jin Joo, our eldest daughter, 18 years old, had joined a missionary program four weeks before and, on that day, the group was in Charlotte, North Carolina. Those attending the program were responsible for raising funds as part of their training to keep the program solvent and cover their own living and traveling expenses. They did this by selling jewelry and pictures primarily to businesses. They worked in pairs for protection. Unfortunately, Jin Joo, inexperienced and not following instructions to stay in the business areas, had separated from her partner and gone to an apartment complex to sell her jewelry, where she went missing.

Her team captain called to inform us that Jin Joo did not report back to a predetermined spot on time. Although she had called in by walkie-talkie a few minutes earlier, saying she would be a few minutes late, Jin Joo never showed up.

Now alarmed, the group captain called the police, explaining Jin Joo's disappearance after her last communication. As some of Jin Joo's clothes were in the van, they gave the police a piece of her clothing to help with the search.

A few hours later, we received a call from Charlotte police telling us that their dogs had lost Jin Joo's scent and they were closing the search for that day as it was already dark.

That evening, we found three brief messages with classical music on our answering machine. As Jin Joo had studied piano for over ten years, we just presumed that she was the one sending those messages telling us that she was okay. It was unlike her, but we thought, "Who else would have sent music recordings? Who knew that she loved to play piano?" We kept a copy of the music recording for years and tried to trace the caller without avail. We have never found out how and who sent them.

Every news channel showed Jin Joo's photo as a missing person that evening.

I was in complete denial, wondering why they would show the story she was missing on the news when I thought she was just resting or taking a break somewhere. My wife, who couldn't bear the thought that something tragic had happened, wrote her a few emails that night.

STF – Special Task Force program

Jin Joo left Seattle as a High School graduate to participate in a missionary program designed to train young people to become more responsible for others and discover how God can work in their lives. Through the program, she would have the opportunity to meet different people, young and old, who would broaden her experience of those different from herself. Occasionally, they would also attend workshops. With all that experience, they could eventually become community members or leaders embodying the heart of God and creating a better world for all.

Eugene, world peace can only come if we can change ourselves through self-sacrifice and serving others, requiring much effort. It is easier to think I will change the world by detonating a bomb, but violence begets violence.

This training would serve her throughout her life and is an activity that would help her in her future marriage, as she would learn to overcome selfishness and put others before herself, a critical trait when one is responsible for a family.

Many of us have experienced family breakdowns when the father or mother hasn't learned this valuable lesson and only thinks about their needs. We also know that children suffer the most from the separation of their parents.

Two days before her disappearance, my office coworker, Joe, experienced a significant stroke in front of me at the office, so I decided to visit him in the hospital that evening.

Of course, I was concerned about Jin Joo, but my mind couldn't conceive that there could be a problem with her disappearance. Joe had been stabbed in the heart while fundraising for the movement years before and was lucky he was across the road from a hospital and lived to tell that story. After many years, scar tissue from that injury was finally released, causing a major stroke. As a result of the stroke, he lost some of his communication skills and now struggles to have a normal conversation.

When I came home that evening, I became more worried and concerned as we watched the news showing a photo of our missing daughter.

All the program participants had to call their parents every Sunday afternoon. Jin Joo had called us three days earlier. We talked for over half an hour. She explained that STF was the right place for her because her heart grew so much by exposure to new cultures and people. She loved being with the other team members. I explained that the most important lesson was to develop her heart and learn to love others.

I told her not to worry about college until later because true education is about learning to love others. Through the experience on STF, it would no longer be just theory but practicing to serve and live for others. She listened and thanked me, then told me she loved me. Little did I know that this would be my last conversation with her.

We never know when we will last speak to or hug our loved ones. We didn't spend enough time together with Jin Joo before she left for the STF because she was so busy preparing. The time for her to go quickly came and she was gone.

The news was terrible

The next day, we still had not received any word from Jin Joo, so I went to work. It was impossible to believe that something terrible had happened to her. I was expecting only good news.

At about 10:00 a.m., I felt I should go back home to be with Izabela because by then I was worried. After arriving home our pastor called, crying and told me Jin Joo's body had been found in an abandoned apartment of the complex. Those words will always remain with me until the day I die.

He had just seen it on the news. Nothing can prepare a parent for such shocking news. She was only eighteen – too young to die – and this was impossible to believe.

Izabela was beside me and we hugged each other, hoping it wasn't true. I called our three other children to come into the bedroom. They knew we'd had bad news. We sat together and I said I was sorry, but somebody had killed Jin Joo. The eldest started screaming at the top of her lungs. I tried to comfort her. I told them we must determine to get through this together because this would be the only way to survive as a family.

Within ten minutes, the police came to the door to give us the bad news. Our children were crying in disbelief. I told them that we already knew that Jin Joo was found.

Then, the local news channel knocked on the door. I told them that we couldn't talk right then. He was asking for an interview. I couldn't believe they could be so insensitive. I knew I had to compose myself quickly because my family had suffered the worst blow and I was the one who had to give them strength.

We were so shocked that this could happen to Jin Joo, who was so good and innocent. It was just unbelievable. I tried to pull out every experience from my past that could help me cope with such staggering and unbearable pain as it became more evident that this was real. It was not a bad dream, but this was happening to our family – we would no longer be the same. How could we ever get over this? How could we ever laugh and be happy again?

A father finds his daughter killed in a car accident

I had given a sermon in Kodiak many years before about being grateful to God. I had been moved to tears by a story I had read that week and shared that Sunday morning while filling in for our absent pastor.

It was the story of a New Zealander who had been traveling home from a meeting. His daughter had left earlier in her car. Upon rounding a corner, he came upon a severe accident. There were ambulances and a scene of destruction. He realized that one of the cars was his daughter's car. He rushed up to find his daughter lying dead on the road. Before all those at the scene, he prayed to God and thanked him for the blessing of life, especially for this beautiful child and the gift he had been given, even for a short time.

This story came back to me and I knelt before God and thanked him for the blessings he had bestowed upon us. I thanked our Heavenly Father for giving us Jin Joo. She was our first child, so it made her very special. During the eighteen years of her life, we had learned so much from her good and beautiful heart.

Our whole community rallied behind us. Our house was full of people praying for Jin Joo. I was deeply moved when friends would arrive to kneel before her picture and pray for her and our family. My heart went out to those who had lost their child and suffered alone, to those who didn't understand or believe in the next world of spirit.

Flying to Charlotte

The next day, we traveled by plane to Charlotte, North Carolina, to bring Jin Joo's body back to Seattle.

As we got on the plane, there was a feeling of absolute terror. My heart was shattered, but I was trying to be strong for Izabela and myself.

How could I face what we had to do in Charlotte? How could we have the strength to see our daughter lying dead in a morgue?

The greatest fear of any parent was waiting for us in Charlotte.

A mentally challenged son

We sat in front of a father with his teenage, mentally disabled son. He was a talker and just wouldn't stop. I thought, *"Oh God, this is going to be a miserable trip with him jabbering behind us all the way there."*

I felt there must be something to learn from this – surely it wasn't a coincidence – so I started listening.

He was a young man of about 18. He loved his father so much and it was comical but, at the same time, a profound journey as I listened to him speak to his father.

His father was a very calm and patient man – a good father.

> *Dad, we are going to move soon.*
>
> *Dad, we are waiting for someone else to come in?*
>
> *Dad, we are moving.*
>
> *Dad, we're in the air.*
>
> *Dad, I'm not that comfortable.*
>
> *Dad, I want to get out now.*
>
> *Dad, I don't like the food.*
>
> *Dad, I am worried. I hope we don't crash.*
>
> *Dad, can I lay my head on your shoulder?*

This monologue went on for the whole trip.

I realized this was the heart of every child. Everyone needs his parents to love them and make them feel secure. These were the thoughts of every child being verbalized by this young man. My heart went out to all the children whose parents were absent in their lives.

How few parents realize the great blessing and responsibility when their child is born?

I felt sorry for Jin Joo. I am sure I wasn't enough of the parent that she needed. My mind went to all the special times that we spent together.

Sitting on the curb

My earliest childhood memory was crying in the dark on a curb outside our house. I must have been waiting for my father to come home and was alone for some reason. He did finally appear, walking down the street to me. I remember he never hugged or tried to console me.

Unfortunately, this was the emotion I experienced my whole life growing up. He was distant and I don't remember receiving any embrace from him. His father worked as a chief engineer on merchant ships, taking him away from the family for long periods. When his father returned, he asked his mother who the man was who came to the house. Unfortunately, he didn't have a father who showed him how to love his children. I tried to be a better father to my children.

But now, realizing that Jin Joo had passed, I regretted not spending more time with her while she was growing up. I wanted to relive our time together. My life in Kodiak was busy. I had taken my job very seriously and neglected the family to an extent.

Charlotte

We arrived in Charlotte exhausted in the late evening. We hadn't slept since finding out about Jin Joo. I would keep waking up, thinking and hoping this was all a bad dream.

Friends drove us to the apartment complex where Jin Joo's body was discovered that morning. It was getting late, but still people had waited for our arrival. They had gathered earlier to pray and hold a prayer vigil where she died.

People in a circle held candles and sang in an open field. They surrounded a picture of Jin Joo on the grass. We knelt before everyone and I prayed for her and offered her back to God.

We were told that a young African American man had killed her. Several young black women came to pray with us. We hugged one another as strangers, but I could feel their hearts of concern for us.

In my mind, I thought about how some African Americans still feel resentment toward white people and are unable to forgive them because of the history of slavery and the prejudice that was experienced. The TV media came and asked for an interview. I told them that one of the girls I had hugged said this is how heaven is black, yellow, and white together.

One of our friends, a pastor in Seattle, saw that interview on local TV news and couldn't believe what he heard. A white man, the father of a murdered daughter, was forgiving the killer. That was unheard of even in the Christian community.

Throughout history, it has unfortunately always taken the death of a special person to change the hearts of the people of the time.

Searching through her belongings

The police gave us Jin Joo's duffel bag, the only bag she could take when she left home in Seattle to start the two-year missionary youth program.

This bag contained everything precious to her. It was a most holy and heart-wrenching moment as Izabela and I sat together, staring at the bag in disbelief. We waited for what seemed an eternity in silence, our hearts filled with grief. I felt afraid to open the bag because I knew it would be painful to see her things and realize this was all we had left.

I took courage, tenderly unzipping her bag. It was a very emotional experience because the items inside became precious to us. This was the only way that we could now touch our daughter. Anything that was hers was sacred. We wanted to hold, smell and connect to her through all these things.

I watched Izabela touch her clothes with so much love as she took out and folded each piece ever so slowly, wanting to hold every garment as long as possible, as though this terrible dream would end if she held them longer. She would again embrace her child – the one to whom she gave birth with so much hope for her to have a wonderful life.

Jin Joo was the eldest of our four children. She had given us so much joy as we saw her grow into a beautiful person. We were very proud of her because she had such an amazing depth of heart and compassion for others. There was something within her that sought goodness and beauty in life. We saw it in her passion for ballet when she was younger, her expression of emotion in her piano playing and written words, her depth of concern for our family and friends. She firmly believed that she would experience true love, which became a strong part of her character.

Eugene, I thought of all the mothers who have lost their children. It was such an unbearable sight to see Izabela holding on to the last traces of her child's belongings. Throughout human history, so many mothers have had to embrace their dead sons and daughters. How could anyone who has witnessed that ever think of killing another person for any reason? Every true mother and every parent, regardless of culture, religion or nationality, has the strongest, most passionate love for their child. This love is more profound than the love between a husband and wife. Tears and grief and unbearable heart-rending pain are felt by every parent who knows the loss of a child.

Izabela was still folding clothes when I found Jin Joo's journal in the corner of her bag. I stopped before opening it because a journal is so private. I wanted to respect her privacy even in death. Somehow, I sensed she wanted me to open it.

I desperately needed to know what she had been thinking about over the last month. There were short entries about her challenges and desire to understand more about the heart of God. In the journal, I found the poem "For My Love." which was written as a school assignment a year before. She was forever the romantic.

For My Love

by Jin-Joo Ellen Byrne 2001

There she lays

One with the earth

Thinking, dreaming, smiling

Her soul is bright

Inevitably shines upon her.

The sun

So warm, so precious, so embracing

The sun flows in her soul

There she lays

One with the stars

Has she fallen asleep?

She has…how tranquil…how serene

For so long, love was not felt

Not deep

Where had it gone for so long?

Found found

She had hope

Hope that now she

Could infinitely and
Unconditionally love
Her soul could now shine.
Like the shimmering stars
Feeling the deepness
Feeling the complete divinity
So passionate
So pure
How it swelled
Swelling of love and happiness
Wholly devoted
Where is her love?
Come come come
She wants to place a sweet kiss
On her true love's soul
She does not see him.
She must wait
Oh, how her heart aches
To see her true love
What they will have
Will be greater
Than anything that

She could ever imagine
There, she will lay,
One with the earth
One with the sun
One with the stars
Her love will grow
Hopelessly in love
One day, her true love
And she will be
Together…forever
In their ideal heaven.

I was shocked to read this beautiful poem. It was so deep and profound and even seemed to predict her death. I kept reading it with tears as I tried to grasp every word.

I realized how little I understood her. Her heart was so much deeper and purer than mine. How could we have been blessed with such a child?

I read a few lines again.

For so long, love was not felt
Not deep
Where had it gone
For so long?

Indeed, the love we all seek is seldom felt. Many of us sense this because it is a desire that is deep within our very being. We subconsciously know that we are missing that love. We long for it but it tragically escapes so many of us. Where will we find this love that we all seek?

This is Jin Joo's favorite quote that we also found in her journal. She had always been one to post quotes in her bedroom and would often send them to her friends.

> *"When you give to and love others, don't think that you are giving to them out of your own pocket. Give out to them as if they were coming from a heavenly treasure. Then, the person receiving through you is actually receiving from God."* – Father Moon

Memories

My mind went to the past, searching for solace and pondering life decisions that had led me here.

The greatest fear of any parent had come true. How could this have happened to one who was so pure and good? This kind of thing happened to other people, not us. It was almost impossible for the mind to accept that our daughter had been murdered.

As I opened the bag, I opened my heart and remembered all the most important and precious times we had shared as a family.

Christmas was always a joy to see the kids tear open their presents.

Birthdays have always been celebrated with a cake and gifts. Sunday mornings were always special when we would get up early and pray together, having bacon and eggs later. From an early age, I knew that the greatest joy and happiness are experienced in a family-centered on love.

I prayed that God would give me the strength to handle this. I felt like my heart was ripped open. How would I ever be able to heal from this tearing pain of losing a child? How were we going to handle the death of our precious child? We had now lost a huge part of our lives. There was an unbelievable feeling of emptiness in my heart. All our hopes and dreams for her were shattered.

I started remembering the feelings and emotions that had guided me all these years. My mind raced, searching for a way to understand what was happening as I grasped everything I believed. There was no way that God had abandoned me now because there were too many times I had seen him present in my journey.

Jin Joo

She was always very independent.

I noticed this when she was about two years old. I had just returned from work and the front door was open.

Jin Joo came out on the deck. I expected her to run to me and hug me like she usually did, but this time, she walked past me with a desire to discover the outside on her own.

Jin Joo loved ballet and began dancing as a snowflake in a yearly performance of the "Nutcracker" when she was three years old. Kodiak had an excellent ballet school for youth. Each year, they would put on an elaborate performance with all the budding ballet dancers.

One year, I was embarrassed watching her dancing. She was about five years old, on stage with all the other ballerinas standing at an equal distance in a line across the stage. The ballerina beside her was too close, so she pushed her to show her how to get in line like the others. It didn't look very ladylike and I pretended not to be her parent.

When she was growing up, I never saw a mean streak in her when dealing with her friends or people with whom she came in contact.

Ballet became a passion for her until she broke a bone in her foot that ended her ballet career when she was about twelve. She was always strong, healthy and rarely sick growing up.

A precious memory I have is when I accompanied her to a school dance where students brought their fathers. We both enjoyed dancing together to classic rock songs. She was also competitive in her way and was delighted when we won the first prize.

She had a calm and dignified spirit, shy and quiet and loved being with her friends. An impossible romantic, true love was what she often talked about with her friends. She didn't judge others, looked for the good in everyone and didn't see the bad. I have thought deeply about this since her death and realized that if our hearts are pure, we will not focus on the negative.

Jin Joo felt a lot of compassion for those people with special needs. Her dream was to help them by pursuing special education and music.

She desired to make a difference in the world.

When she was around five, she drew on the wall of our house. I wasn't happy and brought a cloth in a plastic water container and told her she couldn't go anywhere until she washed the wall.

It was a war of wits and she decided to try my patience, refusing to wash the wall for about thirty minutes before she realized I would not give in and started to use the cloth to clean her scribblings.

Testimonials

Confessions of a teenager

Aug 30, 2002. Two days ago, a friend of mine was dying in an empty apartment. She died alone, with no family or friends to comfort her and no prayer to take her to the other side. Please pray for her now. If anyone in the world deserves it, she does.

I met her when I first moved to Seattle two years ago as a bitter, sullen teenager. She was one of the first people to make me welcome at my new school. A year and a half later, she pushed me around in a wheelchair every day while I healed from a broken leg. She gave selflessly of herself, never asking for anything in return and she always had a smile on her face. She was devoted to God. One of the biggest issues for her last year was whether she should go to college or go on a mission trip. She chose the trip and was murdered. God, have mercy on her killer's soul because he sure as hell won't find anyone willing to grant it to him here.

Her name is Jin Joo Byrne and please remember her.

Jin-Joo is my sunshine

I got to know Jin-Joo in the Chemistry and Math classes I taught this past year at Summit School. Though incredibly talented, she wasn't one to speak up in class. She had a quiet confident attitude that put others at ease.

Jin-Joo was involved in so many aspects of school and church life. She took the challenging and time consuming classes such as chemistry, advanced math and drama, as well as a number of extra activities, such as putting on a murder mystery dinner play as a fund raiser with others in the senior class.

But beyond all she did, I was truly amazed at who she was. She was one of the most thoughtful people I've ever known. She was the student who stayed after class to ask me how I was doing, or to compliment me for a particularly fun or interesting lesson. She was the one who thanked me for the extra time I spent helping her catch up on work, or helping her retake a test. She let me know how much she appreciated a smile or a whoo-hoo! written on her classwork.

Jin-Joo, I hope you know how much you helped me, too. Your smile and your upbeat attitude could cut through the gloom of the dreariest December day. On those difficult teaching days when it seemed impossible to accomplish anything in class, you were there to quietly apologize for the transgressions of your peers, and wish me a nice day or a great weekend. You are my sunshine, Jin-Joo, and I'll never forget your kindness. Thank you for all you've given.

With Love Always,   -Laurie

from the The Real Inspector Hound

Testimony from High School teacher Laurie   *Sept 200.*

Sept. 11, 2002

Dear Mr. and Mrs. Byrne,

    I read the news in the paper, and I was staggered. I couldn't believe it: not Jinjoo.

    I was having a difficult year in 1995, the year Jinjoo was in my class. I had a handful of students who talked compulsively and created a lot of heartburn for me. Jinjoo was one of the good ones, the nice, intelligent, obedient ones who took school seriously and wanted to do their best.

    So it was Jinjoo and students like her that kept me going that fifth-grade year. When the turkeys wear you down, you rely on the responsible ones. I appreciated Jinjoo for that. Plus, she laughed at my jokes.

    I've been sifting through the photos I took from that year. I try to compile an album of pictures each school year. Enclosed are copies of what I have. I kept thinking, "I must have more than this...Jinjoo deserved better shots than this!" I think that Jinjoo was not one of the kids who throw themselves in front of the camera. She tended to drift to the back of the crowd.

    There are a couple where she's practicing falling into Tarik's arms—a thing they had practiced during group games at the Kodiak Baptist Mission that September—but there are few where she's facing the camera and smiling. (What a wonderful picture that was in the paper. A beautiful girl.)

    Somewhere I have about 100 slides from our 1995 Woody Island trip, which you and your son may well remember. I had some good talks with Tarik as we camped out on the chapel floor. When I locate those slides, I'll look for Jinjoo and see if there are any more shots worth sending.

    I'm grieved and angry that someone would take Jinjoo's life. It's an unspeakable thing. It just makes me want to throw things. She was a good student, and her future was bright. I want you to know that she's remembered and appreciated here, and that I'm praying for you all.

                                                    Warm regards,

                                                  Mat Freeman

Jin Joo is born

In 1983, Izabela became pregnant. We were very excited by this news and had prepared internally and externally, believing that the more we could purify our spirit and body even before conception, the better the child would be in all ways.

We moved out of the one-bedroom we had rented in a lady's house and into a one-bedroom apartment, as there would be three of us soon. We were delighted at the thought of being parents. There was a quietness in the house, a peace that lay upon us and an excitement that waited patiently for the new baby. I remember the feeling of joy and concern, worrying about being a good father as I painted a used crib that friends had given us.

We had everything ready when she arrived on her due date, on April 20, 1984 – Good Friday morning – a beautiful, strong and healthy girl we named Jin Joo Ellen. Jin Joo is a Korean name which means "pearl." My wife and I loved the stories of Pearl S. Buck, we both loved the ocean, so this is how we decided on her name. A pearl, as you probably know Eugene, is something precious, rare and admired. We felt that she was all of that. Her middle name, Ellen, was given after my maternal Irish grandmother.

We wanted her to be great – to have a worthy life that could be a blessing to the world.

It was unusual for it to snow in Kodiak in late April, but there was a light dusting on the ground that morning when she arrived. A belated placenta caused Izabela to bleed so much that a transfusion was necessary. My wife had turned white and yellow, so we had to move quickly.

I told the hospital I didn't want to use hospital blood because I was worried about AIDS. The hospital blood bank was tested only for hepatitis, not for AIDS yet. I started to search in our community for someone with a blood type compatible with Izabela's and two friends volunteered to give blood to save her life. I felt so grateful for modern medicine because she would have died if it had been earlier in the century.

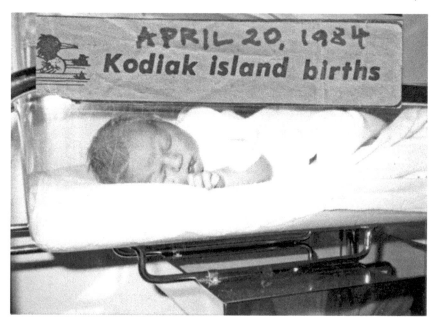

Picture taken by Izabela on the third day of her life.

I had just seen an incredible miracle: the birth of our first child. The intensity of that morning was so great and exciting I still remember coming out of the hospital, driving home and noticing that life was just going on as usual. Everyone was going about their normal daily activities. Few knew or cared that she had been born. I realized this is the cycle of life, birth and death.

To come home with a new baby is an incredibly rich experience, a feeling of holiness and completion because this has always been our dream – to have children and create a family.

This was to be a new chapter in our lives and I was filled with overwhelming emotion standing and looking at her in that crib. I wanted to give her everything so she could have a happy life.

I returned to the present painful reality and could not allow myself to think that Jin Joo could be gone to the realm of spirit. Our family life had been hectic, having three more children in the six years after she was born. There was so much more of life that I still wanted to share with her. I had looked forward to being a grandfather and seeing her with her children because she was a natural mother. She seemed to have much patience, love and a powerful desire for a happy family. I thought about how I had taken life for granted in our precious times together.

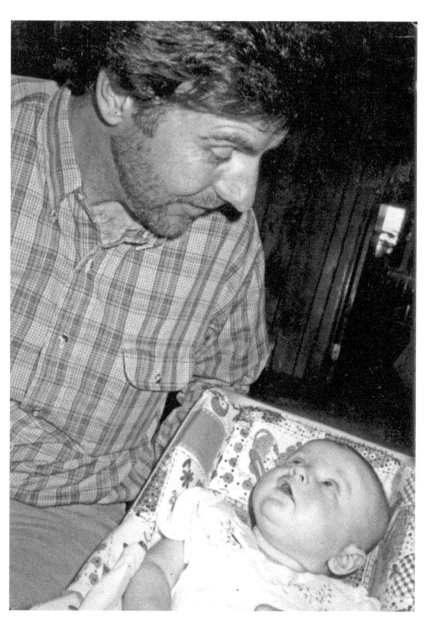

Jin Joo's checking me out.

Prayer at Apartments

Six of us returned to the apartments the next day to pray outside the abandoned apartment where Jin Joo died. We felt a holy presence with us as we bowed our heads. Pastor Phillip cried out in prayer.

As he was praying, I could hear stamping and shuffling from the others in the group.

I thought, What is wrong with them making so much noise during prayer time?

They didn't stop stamping.

At the end of the prayer, I noticed black ants all over David's pants. They had been standing on a fire ant hill and they had crawled up and were biting their legs.

As they tried to overcome the biting ants during prayer, they both looked up and a bunch of pink and white balloons flew over our heads. They would never have seen this if the ants hadn't attacked.

We felt that this was a sign from Jin Joo that she was with us in spirit.

A poster of an Indian Chief and the Ten Indian Commandments

That evening, we were welcomed to stay at Christine and Kurtly's house in Charlotte. They have been such an amazing support over the years. We love them dearly.

I had been lying awake for hours, trying to take in everything happening to us.

As I lay awake in the early morning light, a picture of an Indian chief on the wall became clearer. He sat on a grassy slope looking out over a lush valley, holding a peace pipe, looking to be at one with nature. I wondered if world leaders could ever unite and smoke a pipe for peace.

For the few days I was there, I would look at that picture and wonder what it must have been like when they rode the plains, hunted and lived off the land.

Were they happier to live in an Indian village and be in a tribe?

Even though they were spiritual people, one with the earth I have read how they were brutal to other tribes, the curse of the human race where we can't accept others and try to keep what we have for ourselves.

Somehow, I longed for a community where we could live together.

I had experienced feeling lonely many times in my life and wondered if they felt the same loneliness living together in their community. They have lost much of their culture because their younger generation cannot carry on their elders' traditions and culture in today's world.

I thought about the culture of family and heart, love and service for others that we hoped to pass on to our children. I wondered if our younger generation would inherit or lose the culture we worked so hard to pass on.

Would they be able to sacrifice to help change the world for the better?

Under the drawing of this beautiful painting of the Indian chief, the Indian Ten Commandments were listed.

    1) Remain close to the great spirit

    2) Show great respect for your fellow beings

3) Be truthful and honest at all times

4) Do what you know to be right

5) Look after the well being of mind and body

6) Treat the earth and all that dwells thereon with respect

7) Take full responsibility for your actions

8) Dedicate a share of your efforts to the greater good

9) Work for the benefit of all humanity

10) Give assistance and kindness whenever needed

    I had never heard that the Indians had their own ten commandments. I recently found out that these commandments were made up by a company in 1989. Still, they are wonderful ethical guidelines that could be used to teach our children. Having them on a poster with an Indian in traditional Native American costume would be eye-catching.

    Eugene, youth need guidelines for their lives. As you know, the Ten Commandments of the Bible cannot be displayed in schools. The Ten Indian Commandments would be a good introduction for the children to learn to respect others and care for their environment.

    Maybe The Indian Ten Commandments could be used to guide our young children, as the Indians were the first settlers on this continent. Our children must be taught about the importance of the land, growing crops, caring for creation and living in a community.

    There is a saying: sandals to sandals. The first generation comes to America wearing only sandals. He works to build a business and gains wealth to pass on to his son. The son is given everything, doesn't learn the value of hard work, squanders wealth and finds himself in poverty wearing sandals.

The older generation has a great hope for the future of the younger generation and their descendants. We believe that the most valuable inheritance we can leave behind is not wealth or gold but rather priceless, God-centered ethics. As parents, we have strived to be the best role models we can be, creating families that can inspire and change the world for the better. It is impossible to know how to act and live your life without a model to follow. Unfortunately, there is much confusion now, as young people are bombarded with a variety of lifestyles that promise happiness. However, we believe true happiness can only be achieved when the family unit is intact, where parents love each other and live for their children.

I thought about the spiritual journey that I had taken to this point in my life. Never would I have believed that this could have happened to Jin Joo. We naively thought that God would protect our family. Unfortunately, we don't live in the world God had hoped for. We were reminded ever so painfully that God couldn't wave a magic wand to protect us. Christianity teaches about the last days when all will be healed and those saved in Christ will be taken to heaven. I believe that God is waiting for us to change ourselves and the world here on Earth through absolute goodness and hard work.

It is a mistake to wait for God to intervene in the affairs of the world, so we have to change ourselves and work to improve society to protect our precious children.

Calling my Father

I never imagined calling my parents to tell them such terrible news. I had always prayed for the protection of my family in New Zealand and worried that they would call me one day with bad news. My father answered the phone and I asked if my mother was home. She was being driven up north and would arrive in a few hours.

Jin Joo with her grandfather.

I said, "Dad, I am sorry. I have terrible news. Jin Joo has been killed. She was murdered."

Jin Joo with her grandmother visiting a catholic church on Sunday.

I could feel his pain as the news hit home. He realized then that he would never again see the granddaughter they first met when she was eight months old on our visit to see the family in New Zealand after I had been away for seven years. They also met again during their visit to Seattle and, finally, during our second visit to New Zealand when she was nine. All the dreams they had for her were gone in an instant.

A baby dies

My earliest memories of thinking about God and the next world were when I was an altar boy in the Catholic Church in Auckland, New Zealand.

I remember riding my bike in the dark to get to the church to prepare for early morning Mass and the feelings surrounding me as I entered the church. It was an old wooden church with paintings of the Stations of the Cross hung around the walls. I used to think about Jesus and how he was able to forgive humankind before dying on the cross. I would feel holy wearing the white gown the altar boys wore then. In those days, church services were in Latin and the Nuns taught us the Latin responses at school.

We went to the confessional on Saturday evening to clear our sins and take holy communion on Sunday morning. The nuns had scared us into believing we would be headed for hell if we died in sin.

Later in my teens, I started questioning everything taught at Catholic schools. The belief that a priest can forgive a dying evil person of their sins by giving them the last rights seemed childish.

At school one day, we went to a funeral for a child of one of the Parish families.

I still remember staring at that small white coffin, thinking about death and the afterlife and wondering why God allowed this small child to die. I was emotionally shocked as I watched the parents crying and holding each other. I was young but could still feel the pain of losing their beautiful child.

Another time, a young child was run over by a car and killed. I went by on the bus and could see the child lying on the side of the road. That sight troubled me for a long time.

Every parent worries about their children's wellbeing. I wondered how a parent could find the courage to handle the pain of burying their child.

Born as the third son

I was born in Auckland, New Zealand, the third son in a family of seven sons. The sixth son was born with Down syndrome.

It was uncommon to see people with Down Syndrome in those days because they were hidden from society. My parents were told to take him to an asylum when he was about eighteen months old because raising someone like him would be too difficult. They did take him to the asylum, but after a day or two, they had second thoughts and returned to pick him up. They did their best to care for him and, through this brother, we learned compassion for different people.

I lived on the Whenuapai Airforce base in Auckland until I was eleven. It was surrounded by farms so we spent our days riding our bikes looking for adventures. My father was a Warrant officer in the Air Force, stationed in four Air Force bases during his tenure. Our family had to follow him. We learned to adjust to a new city and school and lived in a house owned by the Air Force. They called us military brats.

I always went to Catholic schools taught by nuns with boys and girls initially until I turned twelve and then to boys-only schools for my remaining school years.

Going from school to school didn't help my academic achievements. It was always hard for me to adjust to a new curriculum. Consequently, I never received perfect report cards.

We learned to fend for ourselves, being the new kids at school and in the neighborhood. I was fifteen when we went to Wellington and lived in Porirua East, one of the toughest cities in New Zealand at the time. I got into a few fights at school and went to dances on the weekends.

The girl next door invited my brother and me to visit their friends and go with her and her father one Sunday afternoon. When it was time to leave, the father was too drunk and unable to drive back home. He asked us who could drive and I quickly volunteered, although I had little experience.

My eldest brother had let me drive his car a few times on the backroads of the ninety-mile beach and I took the family's 1938 Buick a few times with my friend Colin when my parents had gone out with friends. I was fourteen then and we drove the back roads at night and experienced the joy and freedom of driving. Luckily, I didn't crash into anything. We made it back safely. My neighbor said I did well as he stumbled home.

There was another time when I could have killed myself driving. My brother and I had been to the recycling yard to get scrap copper and make a few dollars for our efforts. As we were leaving with a few sacks of copper, we were stopped, told to leave the copper and to move on by the person in charge. As we were leaving, I took the keys from his car to annoy him.

Later that evening, I asked my older brother to come with me and we'd take the car for a ride. It was dark as we walked up to the car. Nobody appeared to be around, so we opened the doors and got in.

I had the keys in the ignition when we heard footsteps and, to my horror, the owner was opening the driver's side door and pushed me over in the seat.

He said, "I've been waiting for you brats. Where do you want to go –the police station or your parents?"

I told him, "Our parents."

He took us to the police station. Our parents had to come and get us. We weren't charged with a criminal offense because we told the police about how he had stolen our copper. We technically hadn't driven the car.

This experience might have saved our lives because I wasn't much of a driver and I could have killed both of us. Or, even worse, someone else if we had gotten into an accident with another car, a thought that escapes youth at the best of times.

All the schools I attended after I was twelve years old were private boys Catholic schools. We wore school uniforms, which I liked because there wasn't any decision about what to wear for the day. Even though we all wore uniforms that made us look similar, we were all very different in character.

My studies became less important than rugby and drumming – my passions. I joined a marching band at thirteen, a great learning tool that taught me how to play a side drum. I wasn't only interested in drumming

My brothers and friends. I am on the top left.

but was looking forward to being with the marching girls. Then our family moved again, so I was not able to drum for the marching girls.

    I have always loved drumming because it requires creativity to find an appropriate beat and it is good for the left and right brain to play with both hands and feet. My favorite drummer then was Mitch Mitchel, the drummer for The Jimi Hendrix Experience.

    Later in life, I did own drum sets and played in a few bands as a hobby. I filled in a few times for a quartet in Kodiak. A Kodiak doctor had heard me play at a church function and asked me if I could fill in when his drummer was out of town. I went to a practice, worried I wouldn't know the music because they only played jazz.

He later complimented me, "You seemed to know the music."

I told him, "Most of the songs you played I'd heard when I was younger. My father would sometimes get a few beers out and play his clarinet with the radio on Friday nights. He had always wanted to be a jazz musician."

I always played rugby for school, except for my last year because of an injury. It was a big part of my life when I was younger. I played as a forward and, after tryouts for a team, I was always chosen to play in the A team. I was nominated to be captain a couple of times.

Friday nights were busy preparing for the game on Saturday, cleaning and ironing my uniform, polishing my boots and washing and drying my bootlaces for the next day.

I also played cricket for a year. We had a tough coach, a Marist Brother, who wouldn't let us talk to each other when our team was batting and if caught, we were given the punishment of marching around the schoolyards on Friday afternoon. During the week in class, we were also given marching time if we misbehaved in any way at school. These penalties were accrued during the week and we found ourselves marching until we had completed our time.

Serious offenses were punished with a cane. My elementary school teachers were nuns, but then I graduated to schools run by the Marist Brothers, Christian Brothers and the Marist Fathers. They all had their ways of controlling us. The nuns used the ruler on the hands as opposed to the Marist Brothers, who caned the hands. The Christian Brothers would pull a short square strap from their cloak to strap our hands.

Having forty boys in one classroom required strict discipline. I look back now at these men and women who had devoted their lives to

God. It was a lonely and difficult life. Consequently, many left their religious calling to return to normal lives.

The Marist Fathers would cane our backside if we acted up. The discipline master was a priest whose job was to administer the punishment.

Every lunchtime, a line of trembling boys in the hallway waited outside his office. Once the next poor sod had entered his office and the door was closed, everyone would listen and count as the cane hit its target. The door would crash open, waiting for the next customer. That was the only way that they could control young men with lots of testosterone. Catholic schools always had three classes for the same grade and pupils were sorted according to their academic level. They always put me in the 2nd level.

My Scottish ancestors

I understand now how my ancestors have influenced my life. They were very religious and came to New Zealand looking for paradise, the ideal world where God was the center of their lives. Through them, I have a strong conscience that has always pointed me to the true and honest way.

Growing up, I felt both worlds: the bad pushing me in the wrong direction and the good ancestors pulling me back to do good. I couldn't escape the good ancestors and finally set my life on the better course of the two.

In my early twenties, I became a lifesaver for the Waipu Surf Club. I didn't go there often because it was too far from Auckland. At that time, I didn't realize that my Scottish ancestors had settled in the same place in the 1850s.

My paternal grandparents' family were Scottish Highlanders who sailed to New Zealand. in the 1850s. Like the pilgrims from England who went to America, my Scottish ancestors came to New Zealand. It was one of the great migration stories. Many Highlanders had to leave Scotland due to the clearances. They didn't own their lands, so the landlords evicted them by raising rents as they desired to raise sheep, which was more lucrative. The Highlanders had no choice but to build ships and sail to emigrate to Canada to finally own land and become independent and free from the feudal landowners.

After settling in Nova Scotia for thirty years, they again experienced difficulties due to the potato famine, which forced them to sail halfway around the world. They built ships again and eight hundred eighty-three people journeyed from Cape Breton Island, Nova Scotia, taking the Cape Horn at the tip of South Africa en route to Australia and then to New Zealand.

My ancestors sailed on the *Highland Lass*, the second frigate to reach the "promised land." She was set to accompany the frigate *Margaret* a year earlier but was caught in the ice until the thaw the following spring. The first boat to arrive in Adelaide, Australia, was the *Margaret*, carrying 140 people and taking 167 days to voyage from Saint Ann's, Nova Scotia.

This is a map of their amazing journey from the Highlands in Scotland to Nova Scotia, then thirty years later again to set sail around the Cape of Good Hope to Australia, where they found it too sinful, so they sailed further to finally arrive and settling at Waipu Cove, in the Northland Region of New Zealand.

The *Highland Lass* departed in May 1852 and sailed for nearly six months before arriving in Adelaide, Australia. It was a challenging voyage.

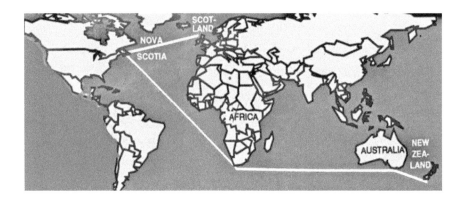

Only a few days after leaving Nova Scotia, a chickenpox epidemic broke out among the children and the food supply of bread was spoiled and thrown overboard. There were 136 men, women and children on the ship to feed. I imagine they didn't arrive in Adelaide, Australia, with a lot of fat on their bones. The living conditions must have been highly uncomfortable for the strict Presbyterians, who were called Normanites – named after their pastor, Norman McLeod, whom they followed.

The others arrived in six succeeding years in three more boats. The community settled into an isolated area of Northland Forest of New Zealand, purchased from the government. They were tough people who wanted to own and manage their lands, so they cleared the forest, built a church and established their farms using primitive tools.

Their story is about hardship, fortitude, courage, comradeship and success as they cleared the land and built their community. They were deeply religious people who lived simple lives and, most importantly, had a strong hope for the succeeding generations.

My Grandmother played piano. Sunday was a day of worship and she was only allowed to play church hymns.

Here is a beautiful painting of the Highland Lass a frigate built in Newfoundland.

My great-great-grandfather was Donald McDonald. One of his sons was Kenneth, who, in 1868, was in the cutter *The Thistle* on a voyage from Auckland to Waipu when it was shipwrecked at Bream Head at Whangarei Heads. He was severely injured. They had to cut his leg off on the beach without anesthetics. He lay on the beach for two days before he could get medical attention, but lived to tell the tale. In the Waipu Museum, you can see the walking cane that he used.

Catholic and Protestant parents

My maternal grandmother, Ellen, was a Catholic and, although she didn't seem overly religious, she always attended church on Sunday mornings.

When my parents married, it was probably uncommon, even radical, for Catholics and Presbyterians to marry. I'm sure their families were against their marriage. That's why both sides of the family never came together for any event or celebration. They worshiped at their different churches and lived separate lives. I missed a family community and knew this was not how I would like my family to be.

My father, Donald, whose parents were strict Presbyterians, could marry my Catholic mother because he had an aunt, a devout Catholic, who loved and cared for him when he was young. Because of that love, he overcame the barriers and fears he harbored toward different religious views. I'm not sure why, but he would never set foot in any church, maybe out of fear of being struck down by lightning, so he never came with us to mass or church events. With everything he had experienced, religion didn't make sense to him.

I am grateful now that I grew up seeing both the beliefs of my Catholic and Presbyterian grandparents. I learned how my Irish Grandparents hated the English, blaming them for the deaths of over a million people during the potato famine. They felt that the English government had ignored the plight of the starving people of Ireland. They could not and would not ever forgive them. I also learned how hatred is passed down from generation to generation.

In those days, English and Anglo families owned most of the land in Ireland and most Irish families were relegated to work as tenant farmers and forced to pay rent to the landowners. Since Ireland was a colony of Great Britain, any Irish (the majority of the nation) who practiced Catholicism were initially prohibited from owning or leasing land, voting, or holding elected office. When times got bad, they had nowhere to go but to leave Ireland with nothing but the clothes on their backs to be treated like low-class secondary citizens in the countries when they arrived. During World War I (WWI), my Irish grandfather said he would never fight for the English and went into the New Zealand bush to hide and lived there for a few years.

I grew up hearing about the Northern Ireland Catholic-Protestant struggle. The anti-Catholic sentiment at that time was very apparent. There was constant news of violence in Ireland in those days. In the 1970s, the British government began to build separation barriers known as "peace walls" around Northern Ireland to separate Catholic and Protestant areas to control sectarian violence. Even today these walls still exist. I always wondered why they would keep fighting about their religious differences. I always thought God would be unhappy to see people killed in his name.

It is hard for the old to understand new ideas – many become saturated like a fully soaked sponge. The young, on the other hand, are thirsty for everything new and hopefully don't take in the ideas of hate and vengeance that will eventually poison their souls.

Although the traditions and ceremonies differ, we all hope and dream of love and peace in our homes, communities and nations. We all love our husbands, wives, children, families and friends the same as everyone and want to see our children having happy lives.

From an early age, I realized that peace on earth could only come when barriers between religions were broken down. I thought there must be one truth that everyone could unite with. I wondered what I would do if I fell in love with someone from a different faith. I was determined to attend a church neither of us would belong to so we would be on common ground. Having different faiths creates separation and confusion in a family. If the parents are not united, the children will usually struggle.

Learning about nature

When I was about eight years old, playing with other kids in the backyard, I stepped on a bee and paid the price for that with a sharp sting in my foot. As I didn't want to be stung again, we tried to kill all the bees we could find on the lawn.

My mother came out, saw what we were doing and explained that bees were necessary for the fruit trees and nature. That experience helped me think about creation and realize that all insects and other animals are essential for the environment.

Shooting a blackbird

My eldest brother had a 22-caliber bolt action rifle and would leave it in a bag in our room.

When I was about thirteen, staying home alone because I was sick, I was excited to look at the rifle. Opening up the bag and peering inside, I could smell the gun oil used to clean the gun after the last time it was used. I was anxious as I lifted it out, knowing I had to be careful because it may have been loaded. I had shot it once before when we shot at ducks on a pond, but that was different as my brother had loaded the bullets and all I had to do was aim and fire.

I found the bullets, unbolted the chamber and slipped one into the breach. It was now loaded and I thought to open the window and shoot into the yard at something. A blackbird had landed on the fence. Not thinking about the consequences, I aimed and fired. To my utter horror, the blackbird dropped to the ground dead. I was mortified that I had killed a bird.

I quickly put the gun back in the bag and went to look at the bird. I never liked killing anything again and now I even take spiders outside. My brothers, on the other hand, were hunters. The experience of being in the bush was exciting for them.

Hunters

Three of my brothers are avid boar and deer hunters. I went with my older brother to hunt for wild boar a few times. They used their dogs to hunt and pull down the wild boar so the hunter could kill it with a knife. A wild pig is intelligent and ferocious when cornered and will come out thrashing with the razor-sharp tusks he had prepared for just these times. Hunting dogs didn't last long if they weren't smart enough to know how sharpened tusks could cut through soft flesh. If the wounds were bad enough, it would be terminal.

I did go with him once to shoot and harvest wild goats to feed his hunting dogs. That day, we shot many wild goats and later found a kid goat alive whose mother we had killed. Everyone thought it would be best to kill it. It was only a day old and wouldn't survive by itself. I told them I would take it home. I bundled it up in a blanket and put it in the truck.

It was a beautiful experience looking after that kid goat we called Jessica. She thought I was her mother and would call out to me as I opened the front door of my grandmother's house when I would come home from work. To see that beauty skip around was a beautiful thing. My grandmother and I fed her with a bottle for a few weeks and then one day she told me she had given her to a relative who had a small farm.

Later in life, I realized that more than likely, my grandmother, raised on a farm, had turned my cute Jessica into a pot roast. After all the experiences of killing goats and wild pigs, I couldn't go hunting again for many years. I did shoot deer for subsistence in Kodiak, but I have always cringed at the thought of killing something.

I became a vegetarian for a few years and started my daily Hatha Yoga practice. I also studied the balance of mind and body unity. My health became more important after a tonsil operation. I looked at how to get optimum health, believing my health could improve given the right conditions. The body is a fantastic creation. It can heal itself with exercise and eating the correct foods.

My first job

My first job was delivering newspapers on my bike. It was a temporary job for several weeks, filling in for my friend who was a paper deliverer. My saddlebags that were strapped to the bike frame were packed with rolled-up newspapers and I had to ride with my knees as wide as possible to pedal. Rain or shine, the newspapers had to be delivered to mailboxes and sometimes I would toss them onto porches.

I always liked to earn my own money because it allowed me to decide how to spend it. I also cut the lawns for my grandmother and her sisters.

During the last two years of school, I worked during the summer holidays at a small factory to save enough to buy my first car.

My vocation

It was my dream from a young age to become a detective. As I left school, my parents advised me that I wouldn't like the discipline of the police force and that learning a trade would be better. After completing a vocational apprenticeship, I could join the police force and, if I found that I didn't like being in the police force, I could return to my trade.

My mother took me to different job prospects. She knew a friend of hers who was a printer and we visited the factory where he was working. He showed me the printing presses and explained how they set the pages for printing. I wasn't interested in that job and didn't like the thought of going to the same place every day to work.

My father came home one day and told me he knew a plumber who could get me a job as an apprentice. My brothers laughed at the thought that I would become a plumber. It was a 10,000-hour or five year apprenticeship and I would have to work in a different city. Plumbing was viewed then as a dirty, low-class job. Growing up, I had no experience with tools and had never built anything with my hands, but the more I thought about it, the challenge of doing something so different became very appealing. I knew little about what a plumber does but decided to see if I would like the work.

I had worked various jobs during the holidays and saved enough money to buy a 1938 Vauxhall car before I had a driver's license. I drove around the house to practice backing up before my driving test.

At seventeen, I was excited to be independent and moved back to Auckland, the city our family had left when I was fourteen. I no longer had many friends there, so I went to live with my Irish grandmother and started my five year apprenticeship as a trainee plumber.

My grandmother cared for me and always had breakfast and dinner ready. I still regret not asking enough about her life growing up in Ireland. I found out later that as a young girl, she had to leave school and was sent to her uncle's farm to work because her family couldn't feed her due to the potato famine. She was nineteen years old when she emigrated to New Zealand. Her first job was working as a cleaner in a hotel.

My first car was a 1938 Vauxhall 10.

She ensured I went to the night school required twice weekly. On a Monday night, I went to bed early after dinner. It had been a rowdy weekend and I told my grandmother I wasn't attending night school.

My grandmother came in with a broom handle as I curled under the blankets and started tapping me on the shoulder, telling me to get up and go to night school.

What could I do but get out of bed in total frustration and go to class? Sometimes, it takes tough love to discipline a young one who doesn't think about the future.

* * *

I lived with her for a year before going out flatting with my mates. I remember a few nights during that winter, we shared a bottle of beer, sat next to a fireplace that was the only source of heat in the house and talked about life.

I asked her about marriage. I was worried about finding a good wife and eventually having a happy family. I didn't want my children to be raised in a broken family because I had seen the pain in my friend's eyes as he tried to explain that his parents didn't live together and he would visit his mother on the weekend every so often. I realized that real happiness can be experienced in the family when husband and wife love and respect each other and learn to deal with different situations as they arise.

As our family moved many times when I was growing up, I noticed the different families we met along the way. Some of my friends were from broken families. I heard about wives and husbands having relations with others. I saw drunkenness and knew that was the tip of the iceberg of relationship problems. I remember saying to my grandmother that everyone should have arranged marriages to solve the divorce problems, but I thought that it was a good idea for everyone else but not for me.

It seemed to me the strong feelings of love and attraction that drew people together wore off very quickly. After many years of marriage to Izabela, with whom I was matched, I realized that we must consciously choose to love and yield to each other to create a happy marriage. We will often have to sacrifice ourselves for our family and spouse and, most importantly, have them trust us and I determined to never lie about even the most minor things. The expression that true love is true is when you can go through difficult times and still stay together despite the hardship and pain. Our marriage has gone through a most challenging time with the loss of Jin Joo. The statistics tell us that 79% of marriages fail after losing a child, so we are grateful to be still together.

I believe my family expected me to last in a plumbing apprenticeship for just a few weeks and return home with my tail between my legs. It was initially challenging because I had to learn to work with my hands. I hadn't worked with tools at all growing up.

My first job as an apprentice was to break holes through a concrete floor. I was given a small club hammer and chisel and told to chip out many holes in a concrete floor as we weren't allowed to use a jackhammer for structural reasons. My inexperience working with tools soon showed with a large bruise on my left hand that held the chisel as I bashed my hand rather than the chisel head.

The tradesmen were tough and didn't have time to babysit anyone, so I had to learn fast and anticipate what they needed throughout the workday. The master plumbers would use the apprentices to get materials and carry tools. They called us "Go-fers," as in "go for this and go for that."

Our company was installing the plumbing for the construction of a new hospital wing. The hospital morgue was adjacent to where we worked. Sometimes, I noticed a hearse transporting a deceased person from the mortuary. It frightened me to think about my mortality.

Life and death

I went to the funerals of my grandfathers. My aunty died at a young age of multiple sclerosis. I visited her several times in the hospital before she passed and I had the experience of seeing a young, beautiful woman turn into a frail skeleton. Her son Owen died at thirteen from a hole in his heart.

My health became more important after witnessing how sickness can destroy a life. I began to study health, learning how to be healthier. It takes effort and self-control to improve one's health. Of course, good genes help. The body is an amazing creation. My faith in God strengthened as I learned more about the different organs and systems. The body is so complex that the belief it evolved randomly is impossible. How the bodily organs and systems communicate perfectly is miraculous and I realized that there must have been a designer, a creator of all existence.

My Uncle, who had overdosed on prescription medication, had never overcome the death of his wife, who had become pregnant before marriage and had an abortion. She could never forgive herself and put her head in a gas oven not long after they were married.

Knowing those life circumstances made me think more deeply about my own life. I look back now and realize that I didn't share with my friends or girlfriends my thoughts about life and death. I didn't know how to discuss those thoughts with others.

My childhood friend, who lived across the road from us, was hit by a car while crossing the road. A young woman I took out on a date was killed in a motor vehicle accident shortly after we had gone out. All these incidents changed my attitude toward life.

My thoughts became consumed by the wonder of life, my mortality, the next world and how I could have a happy, fulfilling life – realizing we have only one chance. I didn't want to look back at my life with regret. Life was short and fickle. I had seen death and knew it was always just around the corner. I realized young that life is unfair and brutal for many of us.

A church-going family

I remember staying with my school friend Chris at their summerhouse when I was thirteen.

We were listening to the radio when we heard President Kennedy was assassinated in Dallas, Texas. Catholics were proud to have him as the first Catholic president ever to be voted into the White House. I understood religious prejudice growing up. It seemed to pop up throughout my life. It infuriated me to think of religious people hating each other because they happened to worship differently.

My friend's family had three boys and three girls, like many of the large Catholic families of that day. I will never forget the experience as we all left in the car together, driving the dirt road to a little wooden church at 7:00 a.m. for Sunday Mass.

The whole pew was packed as the children sat with their mother and father. I was inspired and emotionally moved to see their family that Sunday morning. I felt sorry that my family never went to church together because my father wouldn't set foot in a church.

Although raised in a strict religious household, he wasn't fond of established religion. I remember thinking when I had a family, we would attend church together. Unfortunately, many families are so fragmented that each goes their own way, like ships at night with no center to pull them together.

When he left school, Chris had joined the Air Force and I had returned to Auckland to start my apprenticeship, so we hadn't seen each other for a few years.

When I contacted him, he invited me to the Air Force base the following Saturday evening to have a few beers and catch up on what was going on in our lives. Being invited by enlisted personnel, I could go into the mess hall, as they called their dining facilities. I happened to be the only civilian there that night.

We had too much to drink during the evening and somehow, an argument ensued. I got into a punch-up with a number of the servicemen. I was lucky that I didn't end up in the hospital or even worse and was saved by the MPs who broke up the fight. I was on the floor holding onto another man tightly to help shield me from the kicks I was getting from about three servicemen who had been taught to look after their own.

My friend blamed me for that episode, otherwise he would have invited me for a road trip the following weekend. The car they were traveling in went off the road into a surging river and they all drowned. It was strange how a fistfight had somehow saved my life. I was devastated when I attended his funeral and remembered Robert the Christian carpenter I had met on the job who had invited me to his church a few years before.

Working as an apprentice plumber

In those days, plumbers in New Zealand worked on everything to do with water, even rainwater. Much of our work was roofing – commercial and residential roofing and rain gutters.

Initially, I was terrified of heights. I was so scared to climb up the scaffolding outside of new construction projects, let alone climb up ladders to get on a roof, but I soon overcame that fear. I loved being in the sun and open air, installing roofing and flashings. Our company was one of the biggest in the country and specialized in commercial projects. At times, they employed about fifty plumbers.

In the third year of my apprenticeship, I was the lead plumber on smaller commercial jobs. In those days, all the water and many waste pipe systems were installed using copper. We had to fabricate and braze all the fittings and piping connections using oxygen and acetylene torches.

The company was in the heart of New Market in Auckland and was called Chenery Plumbing. The owner was an older man who would occasionally visit by walking to the company from his house, about a ten minute walk to the office and workshop. He had never married, so he treated his employees as his family.

A vision of me falling

After three years of working on new construction, I was transferred to the maintenance crew, a small team of plumbers who repaired and replaced plumbing and roofing.

The company had three old Fargo trucks that transported us to do maintenance projects throughout the city. I enjoyed going to a new workplace every day with the challenge of fixing problems.

Our biggest customer was the Ellerslie racecourse, the best in New Zealand. It was a fantastic facility that employed about ten full-time gardeners who kept the grounds in perfect order. My boss was a nineteen-year-old who was a little rotund. He looked not unlike a leprechaun with his belly that hung over his shortie shorts, which he wore most of the year, with long reddish flowing hair, a red beard and no mustache.

We became good friends in a short time. Bluey taught me how to work hard and make money. He had married young and had two children, so he was forced to work hard to support his family. We worked side jobs most Saturdays and Sundays, which helped me support myself because the wages for an apprentice were meager.

He had a wild side. Sometimes, we would go out on Friday nights to play pool and have a few beers. He was too cocky for his own good and got us into several bar fights. We would spend many days doing maintenance at the racetrack, so we saw the horses training and got to know some of the owners. We did a lot of weekend work for the owners and trainers and I saved a lot of money aside from my regular job.

Looking back, I worked too hard when I was young, but a strong desire for a future family motivated me to build financial security. At twenty-one years old, I bought land and built my own house with the help of my brothers. We were raised believing in our independence. Owning your own house was a big step in that direction. I didn't want to live in my new house after completion because it felt too permanent and established, so I rented it out, which helped to pay the mortgage.

One morning, we had just climbed up the scaffolding outside the city library, ready to re-roof some dormers using copper sheeting, which we had fabricated in our workshop using a large guillotine and bender.

While working on the dormer roof, my boss envisioned me falling off backward from the top of the scaffolding. He became white as a ghost and trembled as he told me he had a vivid and clear vision. We were both a little shaken and decided to pack up our tools and leave the job site for the day as we thought it was a premonition of a possible bad outcome if we stayed.

Eugene, that experience made me think I could die at any time.

I thought about the next world and needed to understand what happens to the spirit when we die. I felt that I was unprepared for life in the next world if there was a continuation of the soul's existence. It was another step to delve into the spiritual voyage.

The Wizard

We meet special people through divine intervention or sheer chance. I decided it was the former when a friend and I took a few weeks off and traveled to the South Island of New Zealand. I was around twenty-four years old.

We happened to be in Christchurch during midday and came upon the Wizard standing on a box in the square dressed in a loin cloth like a prophet straight out of the Old Testament.

Many office people would come down for lunch to hear him speak. He was eloquent and made many good points about life in general. We were all standing, listening. At one point in his speech, he directed his gaze at me and said, "They term the name dope for marijuana for a reason because it will make you dopey if you smoke it."

I felt that God was talking directly to me through this man. I knew deep down that he was right. God created this world for us to enjoy and we didn't need to be intoxicated or drugged to find happiness. Many people I knew had great ideas but couldn't accomplish much because they were taking drugs, which created a separation between the spiritual mind and the physical body. Their lives were spent in a false reality.

My friends had left New Zealand a few years before and I couldn't go because I wanted to finish my apprenticeship. They returned from

Australia as hippies with long hair and beards and introduced me to marijuana. Eventually, we moved into an old bungalow and lived the commune hippie lifestyle. They would sometimes go together to the country on a bus converted into a camper to take an LSD trip, but I always declined when invited.

The only drug I used was marijuana. I only smoked it for about four years, hardly ever during the work week.

In those days, possessing pot was illegal and, if caught in possession, the penalties were severe, making it very difficult to purchase. There were months of sobriety, waiting for someone to show up with a stash. I became addicted to pot and it was hard to stop. Some of my friends smoked and I was offered it if they had some when I visited.

I had decided it wasn't good for my health or my psyche, so I started a process to give it up. I also thought about future children and didn't want to damage my genes and pass on anything that would weaken them. With those thoughts, I did come clean and never smoked again.

Marijuana today is much more potent than it was then and hospitals are seeing people coming in with psychotic episodes that affect them for their whole life. I have learned throughout my life that if we go against nature by taking that which is harmful to the body, we will pay through either physical or mental health problems. Marijuana also destroys the immune system, weakening the body against viruses.

Many of the Eastern spiritual teachings aim to bring the mind and body into unity. Many people's lives are in constant chaos and confusion because of the drugs and alcohol they take, finding themselves unable to follow through with any plan for their lives.

I always told my children, as we drove by someone begging on a corner or drunk in a gutter, that "they were once young like you with a great future ahead of them and that was the sad choice they made for their lives."

Falling in love

I had the experience of falling deeply in love with a young woman.

One evening, I was driving with my friend and we picked up two young women hitchhiking. It was dark and I couldn't see their faces as they got into the back of the car. We started talking and one of them laughed – I immediately fell in love.

I'd had girlfriends before, but I realized I had never felt love. My whole being was jolted and my heart raced. How could I be in love with someone I haven't seen yet?

We stopped by a park and talked. The girls were in the back seat and it was a cold winter night.

I started to draw on the fogged-up windshield while we spoke. I had never drawn anything of substance and to my amazement, I drew a landscape of mountains and trees.

My friend said he didn't know I was an artist. Because I had fallen in love, all that was hidden deep in my being was being expressed.

I went out with her several times and the more I got to know her, the more I fell in love, but I didn't have any confidence I could marry and stay with one woman my whole life. I had seen people I had worked with who were married and still chased after other women.

I wasn't ready for a committed relationship because I wanted to travel and see the world. It was tough not to pursue someone I loved and I missed her when we weren't together. I learned how terribly painful it is to be lovesick – my whole being was shattered and it was a challenge to overcome for many years. I had to go and explore the world before I could hope to have a successful marriage and a happy family. I was twenty-four years old and some of my friends were married, but I wanted to be free and experience more about life before taking that step.

I sacrificed a love I thought was real, yet later, I realized I didn't know much about her. Love is blind and that strong attraction was only a feeling, a vibrating power that drew my heart to hers. Now, after many years of marriage, I know that true love is the act of loving and even sacrificing oneself for another person with all of their shortcomings. I have thought about her occasionally and wondered how my life would have been if I had married her.

I had a deep thirst in my very being to know more about life and the universe and I had to follow that quiet voice that whispered, telling me there was more to learn. I had to choose which fork in the road to take and decided on the one path unknown to many. It hasn't been easy to find God's true heart. In that search, I have encountered many experiences while living a radical lifestyle compared to others and I have noticed that God has been with me along the way.

The experience of a first love affected my love for my wife when we first met. My heart had already touched another and given its sweet fragrance and it took time to heal and recover. The heart of each person is tender and wants to find true love. I don't think anyone wants to see that true love shared with others. The heart is so sensitive and fragile that having other partners destroys the potential for true love. I imagine many marriages fall apart because of a love that they experienced before.

It takes a lot of work from both parties, but love grows over time. My wife and I are different characters, but we have grown more alike as we learn to accept our differences and to love and forgive each other. I am grateful for my wife's unconditional love because she helped me to change my character. She gave birth and raised our four children, who have been a great joy and enriched my life.

We miss Jin Joo terribly and are grateful we had three other children who kept us going as we raised them to adulthood. At the time of Jin Joo's death, our second daughter was fifteen, the younger daughter fourteen. Our youngest child, a son, was twelve. They have suffered greatly at the loss of their eldest sister.

We all will live with a great emptiness through our lives without her.

Australia

When I returned from traveling across Australia before my journey to the USA, I went to greet my paternal Grandmother, who, in her later years, lived in the downstairs apartment in my parents' house.

She got up from her rocking chair, looked me in the eye and said the prodigal son had returned, but she didn't mention preparing the fatted calf. She probably thought I had been living a wild life in Australia, but little did she know it was far from that.

I had left New Zealand fifteen months earlier, taking clothes and a bag of tools, working as a plumber, mainly in Sydney and Perth – about six months in each city. Flatmating was popular then and it was easy to find a place to stay and share a house with others, an excellent way to get to know new people in a city where you didn't have friends. As you can imagine, this was a learning experience about people. I stayed briefly in Adelaide and traveled to Darwin in the north looking for work, but jobs were scarce. My life in Australia was a spiritual but lonely experience. It gave me time to think and prepare for the next journey, as I now had more confidence that I could travel anywhere by myself.

When I first arrived in Perth after working in Sydney, I lived in a youth hostel where young travelers coming or going to Southeast Asia would stay for a few days. It was trendy then to travel to Europe through Asia. We called it the overland trail. Others called it the Hippie trail.

I also thought about traveling the trail but changed my mind when I saw those returning to Australia sick with dysentery and hearing there was a lot of drug use, which I was trying to avoid.

I got to know a guy in the hostel and we went out for a beer and talked about religion. During the conversation, he mentioned that the Romans murdered Jesus, which got me thinking about the death of Jesus. It didn't seem logical that Jesus came to die for our sins. I started questioning the story about his death on the cross and wondered what would have happened if he had lived.

Seals & Crofts

A favorite duo of mine was Seals & Crofts – their music had a spiritual quality. Family and the coming together of blacks and whites was their message, as they were of the Baha'i Faith.

I loved their music and a sense of goodness and joy enveloped their songs. I did take my ten-year-old youngest brother to their concert just before I left for America. Good music has always opened my heart.

They wrote the song "Unborn Child" years later. It was a

controversial song about abortion that wasn't played on the radio again after its release and their music career was forever damaged.

I believe their song, "Hummingbird," was about the coming of the Messiah and how humankind was waiting for the time of his arrival.

My mom loved America

My mother always talked about how great the Yanks were.

During World War II (WWII), troop carriers stopped off in New Zealand on their way back to America. My mother was eighteen then and went to the Auckland docks with her girlfriends to see the ships arrive with young soldiers. The men looked beat up, still dirty and unshaven, tired of war as they had been fighting in Southeast Asia against the Japanese. She and her friend were interested in seeing men because many young New Zealanders had gone to war. My father, whom she had not yet met, was a Morse code operator during the battle against the Japanese army in the Solomon Islands.

The next day was different as the GIs were all cleaned up and dressed in their best uniforms as they went about the city. Mom always told me how polite they were to everyone. Many were young men off the farms and small towns of America. They were the best of the best, raised with manners and integrity and many of their comrades had given their lives for our freedom. She never forgot that these young men saved the Pacific countries from an invasion by the Japanese.

My mother did meet and fall in love with a Marine and nearly married him. My Grandmother hid the letters he sent after returning to the USA. My mother never knew that he had written to her, so that "love of her life" was lost but never forgotten. She kept a picture of him until the last day of her life. I don't know why, but she showed me his photo the last time I saw her. I understood how a first love is never forgotten.

After she passed, I cleaned my parents' room and found that photo hidden under the doily on top of her dresser. His name was Paul Martin. Because of this story of my mother falling in love after the war, I became fascinated with America. I especially loved the music, the classic cars and the culture – and I was interested in American Indian culture and history.

Coming to America

I returned from Australia with questions about whether I should go to America. I had completed a five-year apprenticeship in plumbing. I passed my trade certificate, allowing me to start my own business, which I did for several years before going to Australia. I had built my own house. These were the physical things I had accomplished, but my soul was empty and not at peace. Since leaving home at seventeen, I had gained more self-confidence that I could do almost anything I wanted if I put my mind and heart to it. Like Siddhartha in the book by Herman Hesse, I thought it was time to devote myself to the spiritual calling.

I read the book *Sidhartha* while searching for meaning and truth, so it struck a chord. I also felt there was so much more to learn and know about life. This story helped me to decide on the even greater need to abandon the comfortable life I was living and go somewhere completely different. I could have started my plumbing business again as I had when I completed my apprenticeship, but I had to make a complete change like Siddhartha: I went on a spiritual journey of self-discovery.

With so many questions in my mind about the meaning of life, I knew I had to be unburdened from the trappings of the material world and break free of the norm, at least for some time. It was a search for enlightenment. I knew it couldn't be found taking drugs, making money or fame. Like the ferryman on the river in the story, I was searching for a simple life to escape the hamster wheel of always wanting bigger and better. I knew that you take nothing when leaving this earth. What is important is what you leave behind when you go.

Like many other young New Zealanders, I decided to travel overseas. Unlike most who went to Europe, I decided on the United States.

Kiwis are renowned as world travelers because they are isolated and live on a small island in the Pacific. Many have a desire to explore the rest of the world. As part of a Commonwealth country, they can work in England as a base and travel throughout Europe, exploring the many countries with diverse cultures different from theirs. An adventurous spirit also helps one get up and leave comfortable surroundings to explore new ideas and places. I wanted to experience new things and meet new people, so I was drawn to travel to the United States of America.

I was twenty-six years old. I remember being shocked as I flew into Los Angeles in the summer of 1977. As the plane banked on its approach to the LA airport, all I could see was a heavy black smog that lay over the city. Just twelve hours before, I had left beautiful green New Zealand with its clear blue skies. Seeing the pollution in the early morning sky was quite shocking and overwhelming.

I was told the YMCA was always a good cheap place to stay for a night. Still waiting to set plans on where I was going, I took the airport shuttle to Hollywood Boulevard.

With my backpack on, I walked down the boulevard to the YMCA to find a room for the night. This was one of the most dangerous places in LA then, so I was afraid and shocked as I made my way to the Y. I sensed and realized I was in rough waters.

It was grim to see the haze above and the darkness of the soul below as I walked amongst people that I expected, would kill me for a dollar. I had never seen people lying on the street before. Prostitutes were openly looking for business on the sidewalk. I made my way past the strip joints along the way. I was fascinated and afraid of all the different faces and nationalities of those I passed.

Security gates were a novelty, too. I didn't understand how to wait for the beep and push the door open. The guy at the counter yelled at me, "What the hell are you doing? Push the damn door if you want to come in." I thought how hard it must be for immigrants who can't speak the same language to find their way in all that's new in a different world.

That night, I dared not leave the room. I felt alone. There was nothing that made me feel comfortable. Here I was in the so-called city of excitement, yet I felt alone, like a fish out of water, wondering if this journey to America was a mistake. I questioned my decision to leave all the comforts of New Zealand.

I turned on a small black-and-white TV and listened to a minister preach. My soul was awakened by his message. If this were the America that influenced the world, there would be little chance for other countries, as the pollution was terrible both in the air and in the hearts of men.

Questions about life had filtered into my thoughts throughout my life. When I looked at others, it seemed they were living as if their lives would last forever. I had seen the devastation of the death of a few of my good friends. That experience made me search for the existence of

God. I wondered if there was another world we went to after we died or if we just rotted in the soil and ceased to exist.

I didn't want to waste my life. It became the most important quest to find out about the spiritual world. Was there heaven and hell? Was there a God who was controlling our existence? What was the purpose of life? The history of human atrocities made me question the existence of a God. Why didn't God rid the evil of the world with one fell swoop?

Those questions overwhelmed me at the best of times and I began to search for answers. The luxury of youth allows many choices in one's life. I experienced the anxiety of making the right decisions so I would have a better chance of a happier and easier life in the future. I realized early on that it only takes one wrong decision to mess up your whole life. I had been searching for meaning in my life and I recognized that those who gave of themselves for the service of others seemed more at peace with their lives in general.

That night, I knelt with tears streaming down my face and pledged to God that I would help him make the world a better place for people to live in peace, harmony and reconciliation. I asked for guidance in my life.

I have always remembered that promise that I made all those years ago. It has helped me to continue on a course that, at times, was very difficult.

San Francisco

The next day, I caught a Greyhound bus to San Francisco. After arriving there, a young man and woman a little younger than me approached and asked me where I was going as I was busy putting on my pack.

Little did I know that they had been fasting and praying that day to meet someone who would listen to a new message from heaven. They invited me to their community dinner. We took a bus to their community house in Berkeley.

On the way, I heard a voice deep in my subconscious, saying, "You have prayed and asked and this is where I want you to be." I understood that my prayer the night before had been answered.

When we arrived, there was a lot of activity at the house. People were friendly and introduced themselves. I felt uncomfortable as we stood together and sang a song before dinner. A quiche and salad community meal had been prepared and laid out on a smorgasbord-style table.

Assessing everything, I was trying to understand what the creative community project was all about. I had heard about communes and always wondered if it was a possible alternative lifestyle that could succeed. The people were all very enthusiastic. I sensed genuine goodness and a real family spirit. The clothes that everyone wore weren't in fashion and everyone wore sneakers. They didn't have the hippie look but had short hair, no beards and most looked gaunt. I felt somewhat out of place, with my beard and longish hair.

We were all asked to sit on folding chairs in the living area. The next part of the program was an introduction to some of the principles that had guided their community, given by an English professor who was one of the most eloquent speakers I had ever heard.

The elephant story

He began with the parable of the six blind men and the elephant.

Six blind men who had never seen an elephant learned by touching different parts of the elephant and described their limited experience of it to their peers. There was much bickering and fighting as the others touched different parts of the animal, experienced different things about the elephant and had difficulty believing any story other than their own. Like life itself, we all have difficulty accepting the views and life experiences of others.

After the evening program, I was invited to a retreat in the wine country of Marin County. Having no commitments, I agreed. I was excited to get a chance to see and experience something new.

It was intriguing to be with such a friendly group of people. There was a wonderful spirit of goodness about them. It was refreshing to be with people who weren't strung out on alcohol and dope. I wanted to find out who they were.

As it was a Friday night, the community bus, an old 1950's former metro bus, was fully packed as we headed to the camp north of San Francisco for the weekend.

Camp K

The workshop setting was in the hills of Santa Rosa, California. The facility had been used as a Girl Guide's camp called Camp K before the creative community purchased it.

I was happy to be in the country with trees and the winding river that followed the road and flowed through it. We arrived in the evening and walked on a long bridge that led to one big central main hall and many small huts scattered over the hillside surrounded by trees.

We slept on the floor in our sleeping bags and were awakened by a guy with a guitar singing songs that quietened and refreshed my spirit. Everybody gathered for a community song and had breakfast in smaller groups before attending the lectures.

The morning lectures were about why God created the world and understanding the nature of God by observing the universe he created. The new truth should be able to embrace all religions, ideologies and philosophies and bring them into complete unity. Now, they had my attention because I had been thinking about how to solve the problems of disunity between religions.

Then, a few hours later, there was a break from the lectures, the hot summer weather forcing us outside as we sat looking over the winding river and the road that followed it. The lecture about the principles of creation excited me to know that we could understand the creator by looking at what he had created. It was like looking at a painting to understand the artist. I had always thought that there must be a creator, a designer.

A random big bang could have never created a beautiful and complex universe, as we know it, with everything in creation having a purpose.

I am always awed when I look at the creation and feel the presence of God in that beauty. As we sat outside discussing the lecture, a car drove by and a young man appeared, leaning out of the window and yelled, "Moonies – you're a bunch of faggots."

I had heard of the Moonies before and had just read an article in Reader's Digest a month earlier. It portrayed a strange group of people who followed a Korean evangelist they believed was the Messiah. I had a feeling of panic and thought, "Hell, I've been conned."

So I asked if this retreat was connected with the Moonies and was told that it was.

At first, I was shocked and worried, but then I remembered the inner voice when riding the bus to the house telling me "This is where I want you to be."

The last lectures clarified some questions I had been thinking about. Nervous still, I decided to stay for the week and listen to the Divine Principle, which I was told was God's new revelation given to the Teacher from Korea, Father Moon, who started his movement as The Holy Spirit Association for Unification of World Christianity in 1954.

My Life Questions Answered

The Divine Principle has three main parts: The first part, the Principle of Creation, explains the nature of God and why He created the universe, plants, animals and finally, man and woman.

Everything in the creation has two common characteristics: masculine and feminine, internal (invisible)mind and external(visible) body or form. If the created beings have these characteristics, the Origin Being, God, has to possess the same character. It was enlightening to understand that God has both of those characteristics.

God created the spiritual world and angels before He created human beings with a spirit self and a physical body. I was interested in learning about the spirit within human life and what happens to it when we die.

The second part explained why God's ideal for man, expressed in the *Three Great Blessings*, was not realized and how evil manifested itself throughout history, creating tragedies and suffering.

The third part describes how God has worked throughout history to restore or save humanity and establish His ideal world of true love, the Kingdom on Earth as "it is in Heaven."

Eugene, many Christians and other religious scholars wonder why God created us and what his motive was. The lectures explained that His purpose for creating was the desire and need to experience love and joy from the things He created.

As an artist desires to see his idea substantialized in his works of art, if his work does not perfectly reflect his idea, he tries again and again until his work brings him satisfaction, joy and happiness. Also, God was not satisfied until human beings, the most developed creations, reflecting His nature to the fullest, man and woman, came into existence. The Bible tells us how God, their Parent, walked and talked with them and they could hear His voice.

I also learned that God could not create the world in six literal days but in six geological eras. This explanation made more sense to me. I was thinking about the long process of growing anything in the garden or orchard before it grows to bear the fruit or how many long weeks it takes for the baby to grow in the mother's womb.

You probably remember that God gave Adam and Eve a commandment that was not kept. My Catholic upbringing taught me that disobedience in the Garden of Eden was eating an apple. Still, I had started to question that belief in my late teens and thought that the most difficult sin to overcome for many was the sexual sin or misuse of love. That fundamental sin seemed to destroy the lives of rich and poor alike.

I concluded that, somehow, the sexual act must have been involved in the fall of man. I was surprised to find that the lectures confirmed my suspicions. The fall of man wasn't the disobedience of eating a fruit but was due to an unprincipled sexual act. That story is confirmed by the Old Testament and many works of art of portraying Adam and Eve covering their lower parts in shame.

My questioning about the Immaculate Conception revealed that Jesus had to have a physical father because God must always work according to the principles of universal law and science He created.

I remembered the conversation the year earlier in Australia with the guy from the youth hostel who told me that the Romans had murdered Jesus. That conversation made me ponder the whole story about Jesus coming to die for our sins.

The lectures explained that there was a purification in the lineage of Mary that had laid a spiritual and physical foundation for Jesus, a sinless man, to be born as the Second Adam, the Only Begotten Son of God, with the true heart of God without original sin.

I think it is vital to understand why the Jewish leaders couldn't accept Jesus as the Messiah, the Christ, the Anointed One.

The answer lies in understanding the life and mission of John the Baptist and his parents, who received clear revelation about who the child in Mary's womb would be and that their son was to be the forerunner for the coming Messiah.

The life story of John the Baptist's responsibility must be one of the most misunderstood stories in the Bible.

John the Baptist was the son of a High Priest, Zachariah and Elizabeth, a cousin of Mary, the chosen family to help and protect Jesus and his mother. Mary became pregnant while staying in their house for three months. Out of jealousy and their family's reputation, Elizabeth lets Mary leave her house without support or protection.

John the Baptist, born six months before Jesus, received an excellent religious education in Jewish laws and became a famous and respected prophet. He led an ascetic life wearing camel skins and lived on locusts and honey.

Multitudes followed him as he called people to repent and confess their sins, baptizing them in the river Jordan. He told the Jewish teachers of the Law that the One coming after him was mightier than him, whose sandals he was not worthy to carry. He prophesied that the One coming after him would baptize not just with water but with the Holy Spirit and "fire."

One day, Jesus came to John the Baptist and asked to be baptized. John hesitated, saying, "I need to be baptized by you and you are coming to me?"

When Jesus was baptized, John saw the Spirit of God descending on him like a dove and heard God's voice saying, "You are my beloved son and I am pleased with You."

If you read the prophecy in the last chapter of the last Book of Malachi in the Old Testament, the faithful Jewish leaders literally interpreted it as meaning that the same Elijah, a prophet who lived 900 years before, must return before the Messiah appears. He was expected to come down to the earth and announce the coming of the Messiah.

The Jewish leaders said that if there were no Elijah, then there would be no Messiah. When John called people to repentance and baptized them with water, the priests asked who he was. He confessed that he was not Christ, not Messiah, or Elijah. He quoted the Book of Isaiah: "I am the voice of one calling in the wilderness, make straight the way of the Lord."

Jesus declared that John was the expected Elijah, but John himself could not accept that claim. Later, in prison, he sent his disciples to Jesus, doubting his decision, asking, "Are you the one who is to come, or shall we wait for another?"

So, even seeing the signs from God while baptizing Jesus, he had doubts that Jesus was the one he should follow and become his prominent disciple to bridge between the Old Testament believers and Jesus, helping Him to be accepted, not ridiculed and eventually crucified.

We can clearly see that fulfillment of one of two prophecies given in the Book of Isaiah depended solely on the human portion of responsibility given to John the Baptist and Jewish leaders.

Jesus' death on the cross was an execution, an incredible tragedy for humanity. He should have been accepted as the awaited Messiah, eventually finding a bride and creating a Godly family, engrafting people to his sinless lineage and showing a model for the world to follow.

Thus, we lost the One who would show us how to live, love, forgive and create a world of peace and harmony.

Jesus came with a new revelation, claiming that he was the Son of God sent to the Jewish people who were practicing hundreds of church laws. Still, his controversial message was for them not to worry about their laws but to have faith and follow him and learn to love even their enemies.

It is unbelievable when all the stories and prophecies of the Old Testament point to the coming of Jesus as the expected Messiah and yet He was rejected.

The Roman rulers didn't sentence him to death as I thought, but sadly, the Sanhedrin, the council of Jerusalem, the highest Jewish authority in Israel, his own people refused to accept him and condemned him to death on the cross.

If the Messiah came today as a man born on this earth, how would the world receive him? Most probably with incredible difficulty. The religious leaders caught up in their doctrines and literal interpretations of the Old and New Testament prophecies, expecting him to come on the clouds of heaven or as a thief in the night, would find it difficult, if not impossible, to accept His new teachings and revelational knowledge.

Eugene, as you know, Jesus promised to come "soon." But why would he promise to come back if his death on the cross was the fulfillment of the prophecies?

How he would return was a question that intrigued me.

I don't remember from my years of attending catholic mass and catechism classes any discussion about a returning Christ. Attending other Christian church services, I learned that Jesus would come on the clouds of heaven and only Christian believers would be lifted up with him, even those who had already died.

Still, I believed all good and conscientious people would go to the higher realms of the spiritual world regardless of their beliefs or religion.

Many questions on religion that I had pondered over the years were answered in that one week of lectures. I was determined to learn more about Rev Moon, who had revealed these new teachings despite the prosecution he was receiving.

Meeting a Christian carpenter

Sitting in the lectures, I was reminded of meeting Robert, a Christian carpenter, when I started my apprenticeship in New Zealand and first began working on the construction of a new hospital wing.

The mortuary was adjacent to where we were working. Sometimes, I saw a cart covered by a sheet pushed into the morgue. I knew another person had died and it upset me to think about the deceased's family. It also frightened me to think about my own mortality.

That experience of working across from the morgue sparked my curiosity about life and death, so I began questioning the meaning of life. Robert invited me to his church.

Growing up, I was searching for a model life, someone who I believed had a worthy life that I could imitate. Most youth are looking for that model. If they don't find it in their own family, they search for it in many different ways. I could tell Robert was a genuine soul.

A year later, I decided to go to a Sunday evening service. It was winter and dark as I drove into the church parking lot. I was distraught because I couldn't get over the death of my good friend. I could have been with him in the car when it plunged into a river.

As a Catholic, I had never been to a Christian church before. I felt great hesitation in doing so, but I needed to go somewhere that night and I had to cry out to God. When I stepped out of the car, Robert who had invited me a year before was standing right next to my car. He sensed that I was troubled. I was surprised to see him. We didn't say much as he walked me into the church. I felt like Jesus had been waiting for me that night.

My life up to that point was not very heavenly. I always felt there were two minds within me: the righteous and the selfish. I often went against my moral conscience and would be troubled later. It was the era of free sex, drugs and rock and roll.

I briefly attended Bible study with that church, but their teaching taught that Jesus would return on the clouds, take the Christians to heaven and leave everyone else behind – a fairy tale belief taught for two thousand years. That teaching didn't make any sense to me. I couldn't believe that a loving God would only take the Christians and leave all the other religious people behind, so I stopped going to that church.

The lectures in the hills of Sacramento answered my life questions and, most importantly, revealed that the Second Coming, the Messiah expected by many Christians, Muslims and others, was now on the earth. These new teachings I was studying were a new revelation given to Father Moon through intense prayer and study.

The purpose of the Messiah was to bring total salvation to fallen humankind and build the kingdom of heaven on earth.

Joining the Unificationist Community

After three weeks of studying the Divine Principle, I started to help with the construction of the camp, working with a small team of guys who were members. After about a month or more, I left Camp K to go to San Francisco to join the "actioner program," where we learned to train in our devotion to God. Many did fundraising and witnessing during this initiation period.

The witnessing efforts at that time were proving successful, with many new members joining the church, but there wasn't sufficient housing for the new novitiates.

I had saved $10,000 working in Australia to fund my trip to America and Europe. When I heard the Divine Principle and realized that the Messiah was on earth, I joined the movement and donated my money to the cause. It was a sizable donation. At that time, a new Toyota Corolla was only $12,000.

I wanted to free myself from all worldly trappings, dedicate my life to God and support the Messiah. Living as a missionary, I had no money of my own for over six years. If someone bought me a coffee, that was a rare treat. My clothes were from the lost and found and I never went to a movie theater in four years.

It was the movement's early years and sacrifice is always needed at the beginning of every new project; someone has to do it to bring success. We looked like beggars to others as we witnessed and fundraised by selling pictures, candy and flowers to shops, bars and on street corners.

The San Francisco movement, which was at that time called the Creative Community Project, had purchased a third house in the Bay area. This house was on Bush Street in San Francisco and needed repairs.

I was directed to work with a small construction team of members to renovate the house. We worked from early morning to early morning with very little sleep to complete the renovations to house the new members who were joining. As we were working such long hours, making plenty of noise, the neighbor, in frustration, threw a milk bottle through our window at 1:00 a.m.

I had always wondered what it would be like to live in a Kibbutz. That experience was similar as we lived communally doing spiritual work as a community of like-minded people who searched for God in their lives and were determined to create a world of peace. We realized that first we had to change ourselves before we could impact the world. The community ran like clockwork, with everyone working together in their different expertise.

It took me time to become accustomed to a spartan lifestyle. There was no breakfast. Lunch was a peanut butter sandwich with carrot sticks and occasionally an egg sandwich. Dinner was vegetarian, mostly a quiche. We slept on the floor in sleeping bags without a mattress.

For those who don't know, sleeping on your side in a sleeping bag is not an option. Instead, you had to lay on your back with your hands crossed over your chest. Sleeping was never a problem because we were exhausted. Before our heads touched the pillow, we were asleep and ready for a new day, starting with prayer at 5:00 a.m.

I imagined our life and schedule were like a monk's life in a monastery.

After completing the workshop training, new members came to the city with a new zeal to save and bring peace to the world. It wasn't like the Catholic Church, where the priests were trained for six years before they could represent the church. We thought we could save the world in three years and with so little training and too much zeal, we made many mistakes.

It was like being in a war zone: there were many casualties and people who lost faith that Father Moon was the Messiah and building a better world was a pipe dream packed their bags and left quietly. As members of a peace movement, we saw each other as brothers and sisters. I never saw sexual problems between members, but there were situations where people fell in love and left together.

At twenty-seven, I was a little older than most and my life experience was very different from many who joined. I was the only licensed plumber who joined the movement in America in those days, as most novices were college graduates or college kids. There were also a small percentage of travelers from different countries.

Father Moon comes to the USA

When Father Moon initially arrived in the USA in December of 1971, the media, politicians and religious leaders started addressing him as Reverend Moon. For most of us who joined his movement, we called him Father Moon or Father. It was not foreign to me to call him Father, as priests in the Catholic Church were called Father.

His early disciples called him Teacher. He taught us about God's heart and how we could improve our spiritual life, emulating the caring and loving heart of Jesus.

He sent missionaries from South Korea to Japan and the United States in the late 1950s. They came to America alone with little support and had to find a way to support themselves. Father Moon came to America because it was the political and economic leader of the free democratic world. Unfortunately, the country was in moral decay, which Christianity could not prevent.

Communism was becoming a significant threat to the world and America was the only country to thwart its rise and acceptability. World peace was impossible if communism gained any more ground.

After coming to the USA with his wife, Mother Moon and his five children, he started to speak at different venues, always having a full audience.

His famous speech "The Future of Christianity" was given at Madison Square Garden to 30,000 people in 1974, predicting the future of Christian America.

"God's Will for America," "God's Will for Man," and many other speeches were warnings of atheistic, leftist and materialistic culture enveloping American land and people.

He called himself a fireman and a doctor who came to this country to save and heal its people. Throughout the years, he poured all his energy into initiating many different conferences, bringing scholars, professors, politicians and clergy to discuss absolute values, the danger of communism and tearing down the walls of divisions, especially in Christianity and other world religions.

There were a number of rallies in those earlier years, both in Korea and America.

The biggest rally was an anti-communist Rally in Seoul on Yoido Island attended by more than one million people in 1975.

Rallies and festivals in 1976 called "God Bless America," honoring the bicentennial year of the United States Founding, at Yankee Stadium in New York City and in Washington D.C. at the Washington Monument, were attended by thousands, brought by buses from surrounding counties and states.

California Creative Community Project

Miss Onni Soo Lim was a Korean who joined the Unification movement in Japan in 1959 while working at the Korean embassy in Tokyo. She came to America in 1965, began her missionary work from a tiny apartment in Oakland, California and named it the Creative Community Project.

Her first convert was Kristina, a graduate student at the University of California, Berkeley, who joined her in 1970. Together, they established the most successful Unification community in America and between 1970 and 1980, the Oakland Unification Community recruited at least 5,000 new full-time members.

Many who joined were later sent to different missions throughout the U.S. and the world. They went to countries where they couldn't speak the language to establish their spiritual communities, where they would often live communally. They were some of the real saints of the movement. In 1974, Onni was blessed in marriage to a professor of English literature who had joined the movement two years earlier.

In 1980, he was appointed president of the Unification Movement in America. He and Onni moved from California to live full-time in New York City. Some members from the California Community went with them to assist them in their new position. I was among them. We moved to a seven-story building just off 5th Ave, the main shopping street in Manhattan.

The same year, I went to upstate New York to work at a new workshop facility that later was seriously damaged by arson. The neighbors didn't want us there. That winter, a few others and I were acting as the security for the property, ensuring the buildings weren't torched again. We took turns at night to patrol the property, walking around in freezing weather with snow covering our boots. The persecution was never-ending.

As members of this new religious movement, we shared a new message from heaven, proclaiming the Messiah's coming on the earth. We devoted our lives to this purpose and our goal was to unite Christianity and all religions. We were in the army of God and had joined to save the world with the Messiah, so nothing was too difficult.

On the streets of New York

Everyone who joined the movement had very little evangelization training and found themselves witnessing and fundraising on the streets of American cities.

Most people who joined were between eighteen and twenty-two years old. Many had degrees just out of college but chose this spiritual path, giving up an everyday life of seeking a career. In the mid-1970s, persecution began when parents became distraught because their children had dropped out of school to join the Moonie cult, a derogatory name that was hard to shake off.

The word went out that members of the movement had been brainwashed. Most families believed this was the only logical explanation for why their children could have changed overnight into a religious fanatic now on the streets of America, proclaiming the coming of the Lord. Little did their parents know these new truths their child studied gave them new hope and made more sense to the flood of idealistic young people traveling the world in the 1970s.

They now felt that the world could be changed for the better, the problems of humankind could be solved and world peace could finally be realized. The Divine Principle was so profound it gave us faith that Father Moon was, in fact, the Messiah. Consequently, we radically changed our lives, giving up everything we were doing and dedicating our lives to God. I look back now and realize that my life and thinking up to the point of joining the movement was an internal journey of thought seeking truth to many questions about this life and the next.

It was worrying for any parent whose child had joined this strange new religious movement at that time because the heart-breaking story of Jonestown, Guyana, was still fresh in their minds. In 1978, over 900 people from the Peoples Temple listened to their leader, Jim Jones and committed mass suicide by drinking Kool-Aid laced with poison.

I felt that I had been spiritually guided to study these new truths and, of course, everyone had their own story of why they joined the Unification Movement. Many joined because they liked other members, but this was not enough to sustain them later. The lifestyle of members in those days was radical. The survival rate for church members was extremely low and many packed their bags and left because it was a grueling schedule coupled with unbelievable persecution.

Most members lived communally with no independent salary. We faced unending persecution for many years as we were looked upon as members of a crazy cult and treated with suspicion. We were attacked in every way from all sides, by both religious people and the anti-religious groups, the communists and our own families. Some of the members were even kidnapped to break their faith.

Our daily life was hard with prayer at 5:00 a.m. and 11:00 p.m. Most of us lived on four hours of sleep if we were lucky. There are great jokes about members falling asleep at the most critical times. It was not unusual to be talking to a member in the movement and see their eyes close and they would nod out in front of you. We were tired but enthusiastic and naively thought it would take no more than three years to change the world, given that the Messiah was on the earth.

Little did we know that this would be a mammoth task.

Belvedere Estate

Members from the New York area would gather to listen to Father Moon's Sunday sermon at Belvedere Estate in Tarrytown, New York. It is a beautiful estate purchased by the first missionaries in preparation for Father Moon and his wife and children to come to the USA in 1971.

We would leave Manhattan around 4:00 a.m., exhausted after about three hours of sleep, to get to Belvedere before 5:00 a.m. Father Moon would speak in the lecture hall of the converted garage. About two hundred members would gather to sit on the floor cross-legged or kneeling, packed in like sardines together, to listen to his sermon.

Everyone wanted to sit in the front row because you would be closer to Father Moon and maybe he would tease you as he often did during his talk and would have fun with those closer to him. He spoke mainly Korean with someone translating into English. They were not the regular twenty-minute sermons given by priests and ministers throughout the country on that Sunday morning but talks that would go on for hours.

I was at one Sunday service when he spoke for nine hours straight. We didn't even go to use the toilet. Mother Moon would accompany him, sometimes urging him to finish earlier because she knew it was hard for us to sit crammed together for so long, but most of the time, he would continue. They were intimate times.

Father Moon often sweated as he shared and tried to educate us about the spiritual and physical life. We were too young to appreciate those experiences of listening to the Messiah. I now wish I had attended more often, but I did have responsibilities that didn't allow that and for all members, Sunday wasn't a day of rest.

He spoke at Belvedere every Sunday morning for over thirty years when they were in New York. These and other speeches are now compiled into an extraordinary 615 volumes. He spent his life teaching about God's heart, the history of restoration, humanity and the universe.

Working on the streets of New York City

We were always concerned that we would get mugged on the streets of New York. It was dangerous to walk the streets in the early eighties. I never had any money in my wallet, but I was never attacked. Most probably, thieves knew I wouldn't be worth the risk.

Someone was attacked on the street in front of me by two young guys. They clobbered him and stole his wallet. I became furious and ran up to them, yelling at them and I chased the one who had the wallet into a car park. Looking back, that was a crazy thing to do – he might have had a knife or a gun! Luckily, he was too fast for me and disappeared. These were our righteous impulses that knew no fear.

The Greyhound bus station was a favorite place in Manhattan to meet travelers more inclined to talk to us than the busy New Yorkers who usually wouldn't give us the time of day.

We would go in pairs at all times of the day and night to the Greyhound bus station on 42nd Street in Manhattan. I went a few times at two o'clock in the morning to find someone willing to listen to an introductory lecture and hopefully go to the camp in upstate New York to learn about the Divine Principle. People we met at those times would come to the church center and sleep over until breakfast.

Eugene, as you remember, I was one of those who was met at the Greyhound station in San Francisco.

Invited for dinner

I got invited to the home of a young woman I met while witnessing in New York. She invited me for a meal with her family.

I felt awkward being in a house again, as it had been many years since I sat at an actual dining room table. Her daughter was interested in me and tried to talk me out of returning to the church.

Upon leaving, she followed me out into the dark, cool night air and hugged me too tightly. Her perfume and fit body aroused all my senses – it was hard to let her go. She was beautiful, but I had to return to my monk-like life, where we learned to control our body and its physical desires with our spiritual mind.

She never realized I'd just had a feast compared to the simple vegetarian food we usually ate. I was never sick, eating only twice daily, but I became very slender. I drove back to the center, thinking about how I missed everyday life, coming home to a woman and a comfortable home.

Deprogrammers

I was involved in a situation with deprogrammers in upstate New York in 1981 while helping at the workshop. One of the staff received a phone call telling them that a unification member was being held against his will by deprogrammers very close by.

Two of us decided to drive to where the house was to see if we could assist and free the person from their captives. The house was in a rural area and the road was rough and dusty.

As we drove past the house for the second time, the back door crashed open and one person, chased by another, ran across the backyard. He was finally tackled and proceeded to struggle on the ground.

I couldn't contain myself as the car slammed to a halt. I leapt out, ran across the road and pulled the guy off the person on the ground, slamming him face-first into the thick grass. There was some kind of struggle.

I don't remember if there was much punching as Galen Kelly, the famous deprogrammer, came out with a shotgun and pointed it at me. That was the first time I had faced the barrel of a gun. I remember contemplating rushing him.

He sensed I could do that, "Don't even think about it – I will shoot you if you try anything. I killed people in Vietnam, which didn't bother me much. He had been arrested in 1979 for assault in connection with an abduction and had pistol-whipped a bystander in a similar instance.

The situation was bizarre as some elderly people were lying in the grass pretending to be unconscious to set the scene where I had assaulted them. Ambulances soon came, and a medical team of senior citizens carried the so-called unconscious in stretchers to the ambulances.

I was arrested by the police, taken in for fingerprinting, and charged with four counts of assault, even though I believe I had only fought with one person. The incident is still on my police file despite there having been no trial.

This event coincided with London's largest libel case, the Moonies versus the *Daily Mail* newspaper. This turned out to be the most protracted libel case in British history, taking over one hundred days with the outcome being a loss for England's Movement. This fabricated story, using video footage showing people lying in the grass pretending to be unconscious, portrayed us as a dangerous cult.

The drama was later written up in a New Zealand newspaper article and I received a letter from my father asking if I was involved, as I believe my name had been mentioned.

I called my parents and tried to explain how the events of that day had transpired.

Father Moon indicted by the IRS

In 1981, I worked in Manhattan as a seven-story building manager for a church-owned property just off 5th Avenue. We had a table with literature close to the library and would invite people to dinner and share about the teaching of the Divine Principle.

On the day Father was indicted for tax evasion for his first reported income tax after coming to the United States, I was at that table inviting people to visit our center and I still remember when a man came up to me and yelled, "You're finished now – that fool Moon will be going to jail!"

With all the persecution we had endured over the years, this was the nail in the coffin, the last straw and it was tough for the members to keep their heads high. We had to continue with the understanding that this was just another injustice Father Moon and the movement had to bear. As members, we didn't understand anything about the tax case and I will explain later about the gross injustice that was brought to bear on Father Moon because of it.

We never imagined and couldn't believe Father Moon would go to prison, especially in America, a free world with religious freedom. Still, the story is a sad one and an unbelievable tale that unfolded.

As the saying goes, the government could indict a ham sandwich if they choose to.

Matching process

If you were God, how would you solve world problems and create true peace?

Father Moon explained that world peace could only come when different races, nationalities and religions unite through the marriage blessing, coming together as husbands and wives. Father Moon became a famous matchmaker and he and Mother Moon officiated hundreds of thousands of couples' Holy Marriage Blessings, called Mass Weddings, during their ministry.

The announcement came that the matching of men and women as couples would be held the last week of June, just before the Mass Holy Marriage Blessing at Madison Garden on July 1st,1982, which happened to be my 31st birthday. All those that were eligible were to meet together in New York. The primary qualifications were sexual purity since joining the movement and serving as an active member for at least three years.

Father Moon explained to us that the matches were not only for us but, more importantly, for our future children and then we would recognize the wisdom of God.

We believed if we purified ourselves as individuals when we joined as a couple in marriage, we could create a heavenly child embodying God's heart and mind. Time was necessary to achieve spiritual mind and physical body unity and fulfill the first Blessing, to be fruitful, to achieve a Godly character, working towards perfection as Jesus commanded: " Be perfect as your Heavenly Father is perfect."

We knew that the second Blessing was "to multiply." but it was not just to procreate but to be able to unite with our spouses, not just "become one flesh" but to have a "united mind and heart." That's how our children could be better than us.

I prayed that I would have faith to accept the woman that God would choose for me through Father Moon's spiritual senses, intuition and long-time experience.

There was an air of excitement in the International Headquarters in the New Yorker Hotel as people came from all over the world to participate in the matching process. The Grand Ballroom of the New Yorker Hotel was packed with hundreds of men and women from different countries. The room was divided with men on one side and women on the other.

Father Moon entered wearing a casual short-sleeved shirt. He rarely wore a tie throughout the years I saw him. It gave me the impression that he would always do more for God than any of us and throughout the years, we witnessed how much he sacrificed for God's providence. I can't imagine the stress he endured taking the responsibility to match people, most of whom he didn't know personally.

Father didn't waste any time. He started to walk up and down the aisle, looking intently at everyone. Sometimes, he would point to a man to come out to the aisle and choose a woman to stand beside him, gesturing that the matching was completed. Other times, a woman was chosen and a man was directed to stand beside her. Sometimes, he would call several women to come out and stand together and walk up and down the aisle, choosing partners for them. At times, he would talk about the person and say things like, "he has a very strong personality and needs a counterbalance." Or "She is very strong and needs a milder man." He would say, "Wait and see their children – they will be beautiful."

That was how people were matched together. Many of the matches were between people of different races, ethnicities and countries of origin who needed a translator to help discuss with their new partner whether to agree to the matching. It was generally expected that you would accept the match. If the man or the woman rejected the match, they would return to be re-matched to someone new. Truthfully, as Father came near, I would duck my head down so as not to be picked.

I was very interested to see how he was matching people. As I watched, I felt more confident in his judgment. He could quickly analyze the character of a person as external features reflect the internal character of the person and the face shows everything about a person's character and life experiences.

I witnessed how Father matched two people who were physically not attractive. Now, I see their children and see how beautiful they are. Father Moon pulled out one brother whose face was disfigured because he had been scarred by fire. Father asked who would be the bride for this man. A beautiful young lady raised her hand and said she would accept him. Later, I heard that Father paid for his plastic surgery. God is concerned with every person.

My faith in God was absolutely put to the test in this situation. I thought, "Will I have faith that God will find the right person for me?"

Father looked at me. It was my turn. He called me to come out.

I looked at him and said, "Father, I want to get matched to an American because I want to stay in America and need someone with a green card."

He looked at me for a while and then called all the American women and women with green cards to raise their hands. He also asked about their age. He looked around and called out to Izabela, who came forward.

I was afraid even to look up when she came out. He pushed us together.

We bowed together with respect and went upstairs to talk. I realized that she was pretty and intelligent when I started to talk to her. I was surprised to find out that she was Polish. I had received an answer through prayer two weeks before that I should be matched to an American.

I told her I wanted to stay and work in America and I needed to be matched to a citizen. She said she had a green card and planned to become a citizen.

My thoughts went to my youth. I had gone to a Marist Brothers private school, where one of my teachers was Polish. He would read us a book called *The Silver Sword*, a story about Poland during World War II. My understanding of Poland was limited until we read that book. My main takeaway was that Polish people endured a great deal of suffering.

Izabela explained that she had been married before and had a child. This was rare because most Unification Church members joined as single people.

All my concepts were challenged as I talked to her. I knew others who had refused the matching for one reason or another and returned to be matched again.

I didn't understand the immigration system in America, especially what a green card was. I told her I would have to refuse the matching because she wasn't an American. We both returned to the ballroom to be matched again.

As I sat down in great emotional turmoil, not knowing if I had made the correct decision, I noticed her crying across the room, which made me wonder if I had done the right thing by refusing the matching.

I got up and asked Dr. Mose Durst if a green card would allow me to stay in America. He confirmed that I could apply for citizenship if my wife had one.

If I believed God was working through Father Moon, he had picked the right person for me, so I put my hand up. Father Moon came over and I explained to his assistant what had happened and that I was willing to talk again to Izabela, so he motioned her to come forward and we again headed upstairs to talk.

I was surprised to learn she was working in Kodiak, Alaska, for a church-related fish business. I shared a little of myself and we agreed to the match and decided to go forward with a Holy Marriage Blessing within a week.

"God comes to dwell in the home where parents and children live in harmony." – Father Moon

He explained that, "God is more fully present in a blessed marriage than in a single person, celibate monk, or nun."

World Peace through the Blessing of Marriage and Creation of the Ideal Families

Father and Mother Moon weren't trying to create another church but a religious family movement by saving marriages and creating ideal families. Somehow, the Movement they tried to create was "branded" in Korea, the USA and other countries as a new church denomination, which it was not.

Our couple was one of 2,075 couples blessed in marriage in Madison Square Garden on July 1st, 1982. It was also my birthday so I can't get into trouble for forgetting our anniversary.

The mass wedding in Madison Square Garden was very radical for most people to understand. Many of our families and media saw it as a bizarre act as we all gathered to be married and blessed together at the same time.

One of the very few positive voices appeared years later from a writer, Don De Lillo, as he described the Unification movement's mass weddings as opening the path forward for humanity. He noticed that the oneness and harmony among thousands of young couples devoting their marriage and family to God was an encouraging sight.

All the women wore white wedding gowns of the same cut, while the men wore dark blue suits with burgundy-colored ties. We walked from the New Yorker Hotel down 38th Avenue in one long line of couples towards Madison Square Garden, only a few blocks away.

It was an exciting day as bystanders looked on and drivers in cars tooted their horns. It was a wild sight even for me as we walked to our wedding.

It was a substantial statement to the world that we believed in peace, harmony and marriage, creating good families and were willing to join others in the international marriage ceremony.

While some couples were matched before, most had been matched as we were just a week earlier. And yet, they were happy to walk arm in arm with their new partner with faith that God had chosen the right person for them.

My chosen wife – Polish Izabela

Izabela was born and raised in Poland, then a communist country, where one Party controlled the masses and much of their freedom was taken from them.

Although both of our ancestors came from Europe and we both were raised as Catholics, our backgrounds were very different. She grew up nearly as an only child because her three sisters were much older and two had already left home.

She learned to love classical music and watch ballet performances and operas. Many movies she watched glorified the Russian Red Army's victory in World War II. Western music was unavailable in Poland and she bought her first Beatles single record in East Germany while participating in an athletic event.

As you know, Eugene, a communist country had a history, economics and politics that differed significantly from the democratic Western nations. All the countries "behind the Iron Curtain" were controlled by

Madison Square Garden Holy Marriage Blessing, 2075 couples, July 1, 1982.

the Soviet Army troops stationed throughout Eastern Europe under the "Warsaw Pact" in case of any possible rebellion.

Food shortages were common as Poland had to feed "their protectors." The free enterprise system was minimally allowed. Few people had private shops and small businesses. Some doctors and dentists had private practices, preferred by the general population to state-owned practices.

Izabela explained how the media, radio, TV and newspapers had controlled the masses into believing the lies and misinformation they propagated.

She remembers her father, a journalist, historian and writer, struggling to hear the news from Radio Free Europe, founded by U.S. officials during the

Cold War and broadcasted into the countries of the Eastern Bloc. The Polish communist government was constantly jamming the radio signal to prevent people from hearing news from the rest of the world. Only partial news made it past the jamming.

After WWII, her family was relocated to Lower Silesia, which belonged to Germany before the war. That land was an industrial part of Germany and all the factories had instructions written in German. Her father was educated and worked in Berlin before WWII, knew German fluently and was forced to help restart factories, especially those that created paper. Her oldest sister became a doctor and the younger sister became a dentist. It was interesting to learn that their pay was the same as janitors or ordinary workers in a communist country. Her mother had to work to help provide for the family.

Upon his early health-related retirement from a factory processing cellulose, her father started to do what he liked the most. For the next twenty years, he wrote articles and brochures and published local newspapers and regional almanacs on different topics, from history to current events. He was fascinated by the history of World War I and WWII on the sea and everything connected to the beautiful nature surrounding us.

He was the first to write about the tragic story of the first transatlantic cruise ship Titanic for Polish readers. He even wrote about slavery in the book Ebony Bridge Across the Atlantic. His interests and creative energy were unlimited. Through his efforts, he purchased a private villa, which was difficult in communist Poland.

As a strong anti-communist, he wanted so much for at least his youngest daughter to leave Poland and make her career in marine biology or any related field in a free country.

Izabela was married before I met her. Her husband was not happy with her involvement in the movement and divorced her and kept their son, who was seven years old. She could not see her son for nearly ten years until he contacted us when he was seventeen.

He eventually stayed with us for two years, graduating from Kodiak Community College. Later, he would transfer to the University in Anchorage. My wife was delighted to see him after such a long separation and our children learned to accept him as the elder brother. Jin Joo, especially, became very fond of him and that's how he became part of our family.

A little more about Poland's history

Reading more about Poland's history, I learned that the Polish people contributed considerably to the fight against Hitler's war against the world.

As Germany invaded Poland, the Polish army was determined to resist Germany's invasion and wouldn't be run over without a fight. They kept fighting for twelve days to hold the Nazis back and show the world their pride in the country. Poland had 1.3 million troops compared to Germany's 1.5 million. Still, the Polish military was no match for Hitler's war machine, which was better supplied and had many more armored vehicles and twice as many airplanes. Unfortunately, more than five million Polish citizens were killed during the Second World War.

Germany had occupied Poland for four years and in 1944, the Polish underground movement tried unsuccessfully to oust the German army in what is known as the "Warsaw Uprising" and seize back control of Warsaw before the Soviet army arrived to take control of their country. German forces fought back to keep their control of the country and as many as 40,000 Polish civilians were massacred during that time as they stood up against that evil invasion.

Hitler was so furious that Poland had fought back with such ferocity that he told his generals not to leave a stone unturned. They flattened Warsaw, destroying eighty-five percent of the city before abandoning it.

I also learned that many Polish pilots joined the RAF and fought for England and a provisional Polish government was created in London.

In 1945, Poland came under Soviet control behind the Iron Curtain. The Poles have never forgotten the war and learned to survive under harsh conditions. In 1980, they established the Solidarity movement, an anti-communist movement that sought to free itself from the yoke of communism and the USSR.

The Solidarity reform movement forced the Polish communist government to recognize it through a wave of strikes. Especially those in Gdansk Shipyard led by an electrician, Lech Walesa, who was nominated in 1981 to receive the Nobel Peace Prize, becoming the president of Poland in 1989. Solidarity candidates won all but one of the senate seats.

Mikhail Gorbachev, the last president of the Soviet Union, declared that the USSR would no longer interfere in Eastern Europe's internal affairs.

Izabela and I were invited to watch a documentary about the Solidarity movement the first week after our Blessing of Marriage. She wanted me to connect to her country, which was already changing towards democracy.

I was shocked to see the Polish workers' weary and sad faces during their Solidarity marches. I could see how the tragic history of partitions, wars, occupations and a constant struggle for an independent nation made Polish people as they are today – proud, stubborn, strong and independent. As I was raised in a free democratic country, it is still difficult to imagine what the people of those countries had to go through.

She tried to explain how people were afraid to speak out if they disapproved of government policies for fear of being taken away, interrogated, imprisoned, or executed.

Living in a country where you can't trust anyone and can't speak your mind must be the most miserable life. The COVID-19 experience helped me to understand what it was like to some degree. Those of us who rejected and believed the vaccine wasn't adequately tested and could protect ourselves with natural remedies were forced to be vaccinated or lose our jobs. We had friends stop talking to us because of our decision. We experienced the bullying power of one group dictating their beliefs on others.

We witnessed how the media would remove anyone's objections from display. This bordered on a communist experience as we felt the mighty hand of the government forcing its will.

The Washington Times

In 1982, all the members were surprised when Father Moon announced he would start another newspaper in Washington, D.C.

After *The Washington Star* closed in 1981, there was only one newspaper in D.C., *The Washington Post*, with a vast readership.

All members with any desire or training in media were asked to attend a meeting with Father Moon. He handpicked the staff from those who participated, most having no experience. The word went out quickly that Father Moon was starting *The Washington Times* and the life expectancy for the newspaper predicted by all those in the media at the time was six months to a year if it was lucky.

Father Moon said that *The Washington Times* newspaper was conceived because the press must be moral and should use their freedom to protect, preserve and promote God-given human rights and dignity and lead the fight against drug abuse, pornography and other destructive vices and also be the conscience of society.

At that critical time, the fight against communist ideology was an ongoing battle for the hearts and minds of America's young people and the free world. Even though *The Washington Times* lost substantial money every year since its inception, Father Moon poured his heart into the newspaper over the years to support it financially and wouldn't give up on it. He contributed over a billion dollars of the movement's funds to continue its conservative and more God-centered voice for America.

Those funds would have helped the movement expand, but he felt it was more important to maintain *The Washington Times* to save America. The word Conservative has been given a derogatory name and it should mean to conserve things that are precious to Heaven – most importantly, the family and the creation, as we are responsible for being earth's stewards. He stressed that the media's role is to promote ethics and moral values in our society. A peaceful world is only possible based on peaceful, ideal families. He felt that the newspaper helped people understand the importance of strong moral family values.

In a speech on the twentieth anniversary of the founding of *The Washington Times*, Father Moon explained his motivation behind establishing the paper. "I founded *The Washington Times* as an expression of my love for America and to fulfill the Will of God, who seeks to establish America in His Providence," he said. "In the context of God's Will, there needed to be a newspaper with the philosophical and ideological foundation to encourage and enlighten the people and leaders of America."

Reagan and the fall of the Soviet Block

President Reagan was a two-term Republican president of the United States from 1981 to1989. Margaret Thatcher was the prime minister of the United Kingdom from 1979 to 1990. They were both in office when *The Washington Times* was created. President Reagan read *The Washington Times* daily and later thanked Father Moon for the support and guidance the newspaper gave him while in office. He said that they fought the cold war together.

As the paper celebrated its 25th anniversary in 2007, Margaret Thatcher said it was challenging for Dr. Moon when he started *The Washington Times*. She thanked him for the firm standing of the newspaper against Soviet communism and his support to President Reagan and me for ending the Cold War.

President Reagan had gone into office with three determinations – to fight communism, cut government and cut taxes. He will be regarded as one of the finest presidents in American history, who ruled with integrity and compassion and set a moral example for the country.

He was criticized for overspending on the war machine, but it may have saved us from a nuclear war with Russia.

His philosophy of carrying a "big stick" and "trust but verify" saved America from disaster.

The Washington Times supported the proposal to develop the Strategic Defense Initiative with Lasers that could destroy incoming missiles proposed by President Reagan.

Finally, the Soviet Union had to give up funding its war machine. due to a lack of financial capital.

Many young members of our movement were asked to go to West and East Germany, contributing to the Fall of the Berlin Wall in 1989.

The wall of communism didn't come down by itself. It was a united front of people and Father Moon and our movement made a tremendous contribution to the collapse of the Soviet Union in 1991 after seventy-four years in which they had held the world in fear.

Che Guevara T-shirt

In the 1970s, it was common to see people wearing a T-shirt with the image of Che Guevara emblazoned on it. Some even copied his military-style clothing. It became cool to look like a revolutionary.

I'm sure few people then knew much about the Cuban guerrilla who murdered many innocent people while helping Fidel Castro and Cuban communists take over the island in the 1950's. Guevara died doing what he did best: fomenting revolution and killing people.

They managed to turn one of the most beautiful countries in the world into a hellhole where people have been trying to escape ever since, even risking their lives in makeshift boats.

Communism

As Communism was the most significant danger to the world's freedom and peace, most Unification resources, spending millions of dollars and human resources worldwide, were geared toward fighting communism in the 1970s and 1980s. Father Moon and the Unification Movement were the foremost opponents of communism during those years.

Father Moon was arrested many times during his student years in Tokyo for involvement in Korea's independent movement. Shortly after WWII, he went to North Korea to witness to Christian leaders and was arrested, interrogated and tortured to the point of death. After recovering from torture, he started witnessing activities again and was reported to communist authorities. But this time, after a few months in prison, he was sentenced to five years in a forced labor camp near the city of Heung Nam on the east coast of North Korea. He endured two years and eight months of hard labor and meager food portions. He and others were liberated in October 1950 by the United Nations forces.

He experienced firsthand how religious people were treated under a communist government. Even today, we can see similar treatments for religious activities in North Korea and China.

In late 1960, he created an organization, VOC (Victory Over Communism), as communism flourished worldwide and attracted many young people and leaders. Japan was especially vulnerable to being influenced by Marxist theories. Father Moon created many training centers on college campuses throughout Japan to counter communism and Japanese communism suffered greatly from this anti-communist movement. After hearing a different spiritual view of the world, many students turned their backs on that ideology.

At the peak of Soviet imperialism, the Soviet government targeted three individuals as their greatest enemies: President Reagan, Pope John Paul II and Father Moon. They feared Father Moon the most because he had developed a God-centered ideology that could defeat Marxism-Leninism movement worldwide, putting communism on the defensive in every part of the globe.

The Unification movement fought against the God-denying ideology of Marxism with a superior ideology through VOC (Victory Over Communism). In 1980, our movement created CAUSA (Spanish for 'cause'), a God-centered movement to protect Latin America from communist takeover. The lectures explained the existence of God and the spiritual world and the goal of human history in many universities worldwide. Thousands of ministers were educated about the reality of communism using CAUSA materials.

Before being introduced to these new materials, they had been more concerned about the Antichrist and expected him to be a person. Before their eyes, the Antichrist of communism was working to eradicate all religions, especially Christianity, that had helped build the democratic world. The churches have broken up into different denominations, unable to work together now, losing the influence they had on societies earlier.

In contrast, this God-denying ideology, which believes in taking power by force and executions, has been united, making much ground since its inception in 1917 by Lenin and his followers.

Eugene, I realized that an ideal society and world is not achieved through violence and war as typical of Marxism and communism but is based on peaceful solutions. A peaceful world can only be realized by first changing ourselves, sacrificing for others, overcoming all sorts of evil through forgiveness and reconciliation and creating good and responsible families.

Communist dictators believed they could create a new world by struggle and deception but couldn't go beyond their nationalism. In the USSR, communism began in 1917. The state was responsible for seeing that all workers and citizens would share equally in the fruits of their labor, but by 1921, the system failed and the United States had to send emergency food shipments to help. By 1930, millions were dying of starvation. All citizens opposing Stalin's rules were tortured, executed, or sent to Gulags, which were forced labor concentration camps set up across the Soviet Union.

Our youth today have been indoctrinated in universities that socialism or communism is good for humanity but without providing individual and family moral ethics and addressing the problems of youth.

They have not learned the lessons of history and as the saying goes, if you don't know your history, you are destined to repeat it.

Over one hundred fifty million people have died in this last century under the rule of communism. Religious people were the first to be exterminated when communism took over because the ultimate goal of communism is to destroy the world of religion, which they have called the opiate of the masses.

Unfortunately, our youth have not understood what it is like to live in a country that allows no freedom – no freedom to worship, no freedom of the press, no freedom to travel, no freedom to speak out and disagree, or if you do, you could be incarcerated, tortured, beaten or placed on a list where you cannot be employed.

The COVID-19 pandemic has given them a glimpse of that world and hopefully, in the future they will stand up to defend their freedoms.

People have become like sheep, unwilling to step outside the flock, fearful of being persecuted by others and running with the pack to their demise. Freedom is humanity's most sacred gift – losing it should be one of our greatest fears.

Here are a few recent examples of what happened in a communist country in relatively recent years.

From 1975-1979, the Khmer Rouge in Cambodia, under the leadership of the Communist party, systematically targeted Cambodians who were either religious or educated intellectuals (anyone who wore glasses), resulting in the death of 1.5 to 2 million people.

In Vietnam, the communists first killed priests and nuns and burned churches. The history of Cambodia, Vietnam and Cuba pales compared to the many killed in China and Russia, where most churches were destroyed and believers were severely tortured and sent to Gulags in Siberia.

Those stories of atrocities woke me from my ignorant youth and forced me to ponder how this could happen in modern civilization. What was wrong with humanity and why has history seen so much blood spilled throughout the ages?

> *"Christianity has failed to take care of the people and the greatest error occurs when people think that they can just believe in God and Jesus and will receive more blessings from God. Such people feel they can have everything they want without doing anything in return. That is a similar*

attitude to a thief who just takes things without working. The attitude that I am saved because I believe in Jesus has made them complacent and they have patiently waited for Jesus to come back on the clouds of heaven and call them back to heaven and receive their niche there.

Man's portion of responsibility is a cosmic truth. Great discoveries have been made in science, such as Einstein's theory of relativity; however, the discovery of the law of human responsibility is the greatest of all. Without understanding this principle, the most fundamental issues in life remain a puzzle. Why do righteous people always have to suffer? Why is a great man's name only resurrected after his death? The answers to these questions hinge upon the principles of the human portion of responsibility." – Father Moon

Flying to Alaska

In the spring of 1983, a year after the Holy Marriage Blessing in Madison Square Garden, I left New York for Kodiak Island in Alaska. I had spent three years in Manhattan doing church activities and managing a seven-story church property just off the busy 5th Avenue.

Izabela has a degree in Marine Fishery Technology from Poland. Because of that degree and her desire to be close to the ocean, she volunteered to work first in the processing fish plant in Norfolk, Virginia, and a few years later in the plant in Kodiak.

I was nearly thirty-two years old and Izabela was two years older. We had only met a few times after our matching and Blessing, so we didn't know each other. During that year, we exchanged a few letters and spoke on the phone several times.

It would seem a bizarre scenario for most of the world and you can only imagine how I felt flying to Kodiak Island. I was going to Alaska, a wild and cold land, to join a woman, my wife, whom I did not know. I had lived a monastic and missionary life for the last seven years and had not even touched or kissed a girl in all those years.

This would be a whole new journey to be with my wife, who I didn't know yet. Western culture always shows romantic love in the movies, but I didn't have those feelings yet. I knew that love would take time and still, I was excited at the thought of being together with her and hopefully creating a family.

In most marriages in our movement, it was customary for a wife to join her husband after they were married. Our particular case was different. The Alaskan company president didn't want her to leave Kodiak because she was the quality control manager for the company, so as it worked out, I was on the way to Alaska to join my wife. I was excited to see what lay ahead as a new adventure unfolded.

Not only would I be with my wife, but I was destined to work in a smelly fish plant, which didn't sound very appealing. After spending the last three years in Manhattan, one of the busiest cities in the world, I was looking forward to being out in nature again.

Once I arrived in Anchorage, I immediately felt I was in another world. The men and women were not dressed like those from Manhattan but were outfitted in a more casual style. This was going to be another story. I would learn much from the thirteen years of experience with Alaska's people and culture in the years ahead and rarely think about Manhattan again.

Kodiak Island lies in the Gulf of Alaska, surrounded by an unforgiving ocean. Many of her best people were lost to the frigid waters surrounding the island and beyond. Many fishing boats sank in the years I was there, taking more than twenty fishermen with them every year. Because Kodiak was such a small town with less than 5,000 inhabitants, people knew many of those who had perished.

There were few opportunities for men in a small town, so fishing became their life. I have always been impressed with how brave and capable the captains and crews were. They could fix everything on their boats, understand the sophisticated equipment in the wheelhouse, do their books, manage a crew of independent guys and catch tons of different fish, sometimes even crab.

On the one-hour flight from Anchorage to Kodiak Island in the Gulf of Alaska, I spoke with the person beside me. He asked me why I was going to Kodiak.

After mentioning that I would work for a fish processing company, International Seafoods of Alaska, he looked at me and sighed, "Oh, you are going to work for the Moonies."

The conversation stopped. I realized that coming to live on a small island would be difficult as small towns can be very prejudiced.

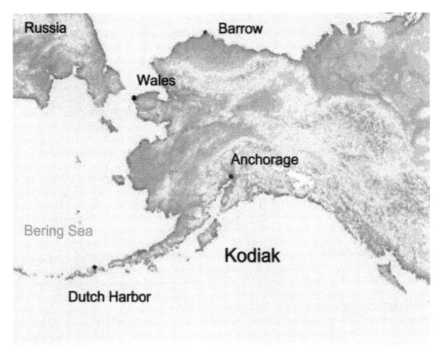

Kodiak community demonstrates

In 1980, construction of our fish company in Kodiak began. Word got out that we would eventually take over the town and control the fish business, a common theme of persecution throughout the movement's history. A demonstration was assembled to oppose the construction of the new plant.

They never realized that we were only a small group of people who weren't skilled at operating a fish processing plant. Over the years, we did learn and found it to be a challenging business to make any profit. Some other fish processing companies on the island had declared bankruptcy or simply closed down.

Over the years, Chinese fish processors with a cheaper labor force would become significant players in our industry. Chinese secondary processing companies could buy Russian-caught fish and sell finished fish filets back to America for less than it would cost us to produce them in Alaskan plants.

Alaska and Kodiak Island

I think it's interesting to know that in 1867, Russia sold Alaska, known as "Russian America," to the United States for the small amount of $7.2 million. It was more for a political reason, as Russia didn't want to be absorbed by Britain or Canada, their enemies, after the defeat in the Crimean War. The only potential buyer was the USA.

Alaska is rich in natural resources, including oil, gold and other minerals. Its waters are teaming with fish, crabs and sea life. Today, its estimated worth is over $500 billion. I am sure that the Russians regret selling it to the U.S.

At that time, Kodiak Island was a center for the seal fur trade market and Kodiak village developed over the years because it was the only port that did not freeze in the winter.

Years later, Kodiak became the center for commercial fishing. In the early 20th century, fish processors set up canneries around the island and a few still remain.

Different animals were introduced to the island, such as Sitka Deer, mountain goats, rabbits and beavers and the Kodiak National Wildlife Refuge was created.

Filming bears on Kodiak Island

The Kodiak brown bear is prolific on Kodiak Island. It is believed the estimated population is over three thousand animals. Giant bears can grow to be ten feet tall when standing on hind legs. They are such powerful animals that can travel at short bursts of forty miles an hour, so there's no way in the world you can outrun them.

In the summer of 1987, I volunteered to film bears with a cameraman at Karluk River on the west side of Kodiak Island. We flew in by floatplane, landed at the mouth of the river and met with Tom, a guide who would accompany us on our travels for the day.

This was the fishing season for the Kodiak bears and we came to film them catching salmon in the river. These were older days when the camera needed a cord connected to a tape recorder that I was carrying. I carried a 45 pistol for safety but was told by the guide that a pistol would never stop a charging bear. Well, that made me feel confident.

As we walked up the river, we ran into a mother bear with three cubs. She wasn't happy to see us and her hackles were raised.

The guide told us it was a dangerous situation for us and that we should make a wide berth around her by going through the long weeds and circling around the creek. We were wearing hip waders, which kept us dry.

Visibility was poor as the long weeds were shoulder-high. To the left of us, not more than twenty yards away, a huge bear appeared above the long weeds as he stood up about ten feet tall on his hind legs, checking us out. I started to feel panic as I realized we'd arrived at their feeding time.

We came out of the weeds into the river and noticed a number of bears fishing in the river. They seemed preoccupied and Dan, the cameraman, proceeded to get closer to start filming.

We were in the river, closer than twenty-five yards, filming the bears. I was terrified. The cord was stretched tight as the cameraman moved forward and I pulled back. We saw about fifteen bears that day and finally had to move when we ran into the same mother bear and cubs we'd seen when we first entered Karluk. She was even more angry this time and started making woofing noises and clacking her teeth like a hammer hitting an anvil.

Mother bears and cubs in Karluk River.

    She was across the riverbank and her cubs were up a tree as she started to make false charges at us.

    The guide said she was ready to charge and the guns we had wouldn't stop her if she came at us. He told us to get out of the river quickly.

I promptly turned back, forgetting I was connected to the cameraman by a chord and pulled him over backward as he was trying to capture the last shot of the bear.

He told me later that when he gained his senses and felt himself being pulled, he thought the bear had him and soon realized I was pulling him by the video cord.

It became another good story to be told at the campfire.

The seafood business

As the movement developed in the U.S. and other countries, Father Moon looked at different businesses that could be established to help fund the different projects that had been envisioned. There were now thousands of married couples worldwide starting their families who would also need a steady income to support themselves.

Father decided to develop a seafood business to integrate the fishing industry, building fishing boats, processing plants, distribution facilities, Japanese restaurants and developing sport fishing. Over the years, a successful distribution business in America developed as sushi restaurants became very popular.

Father Moon was way beyond his time for many projects. He directed research on Alaska's seafood business, realizing that an opportunity arose after foreign trawlers were prohibited from fishing the abundant stocks of white fish, cod and pollock, to name a few, in Alaskan waters.

I was very fortunate to be personally involved in the fish business in Alaska. I found my niche quickly and loved the seafood business because it was exciting and challenging on a daily basis.

He initially wanted to buy a factory trawler to fish the Bering Sea, but other leaders advised against that idea and settled on a shoreside property in Kodiak, Alaska. In 1980, our Kodiak plant was the first to be built for white fish processing in Alaska. We also would process the traditional species caught in those waters, like salmon, cod, pollock, sole and halibut, to name a few. In the next two decades, the fisheries in Alaska would develop into a vast industry. Kodiak was a minor fishery compared to the Bering Sea, which would become world-renowned for its productive and profitable fisheries.

Unfortunately, the movement's elders didn't fully understand how difficult it would be to operate a religious community-owned company in a small town. They soon realized the challenges ahead.

I remember the first day at the fish processing plant. At lunchtime, I borrowed a fishing rod and Izabela and I sat outside on the dock where the fishing boats would tie up to deliver their bounty. I caught an ugly-looking rockfish and Izabela fileted it and cooked it for lunch. She's an excellent cook and has fed me well all these years.

We lived separately in a community house and it was good we had a chance to get to know each other before we moved together into one room of a lady's house. Izabela seemed not to be upset to be living in a lady's house and not having our own separate place. I found that as years went by, she wasn't so much concerned with physical things as she was with her spiritual life and always kept me on track in that regard.

We would go to the company together every day to work in our different roles. We found something in common and we both felt it was our mission to create a successful company despite the challenges.

Izabela, checking fish blocks for proper dimensions.

We soon found out that Izabela was pregnant and I would be a father. Wow! It was great news! She was still managing the Quality Control and Sanitation Department and participated in a few research projects over the years to come.

I spent twenty-one years working for the company in different capacities, taking on more responsibilities as the years went by, starting as the purchasing manager and ending as the company's CEO.

Initially, coming to Kodiak in 1983, I worked as the purchasing manager, responsible for procuring everything needed to run the business, from processing machinery and engineering equipment to packaging. I bought fishing supplies for the boats until they became independent, creating their own fishing company.

Later, we had a group of salmon fishermen in Chignik on the Aleutian chain. They would ask me to purchase everything they needed for their salmon season. Outboard motors, small boats, building materials, engine parts, alcohol and, one-time, hay for a fisherman's horse, to name a few, were bought and sent on salmon tenders.

Living on an island in the Gulf of Alaska made getting materials, equipment, machinery parts and packaging challenging as they were ferried to the island by container ship. There was always a concern that we would run out of something because it took so long for shipping to arrive from Seattle.

In December 1983, three fishing trawlers built by a sister company in Alabama arrived in Kodiak to fish for our plant. They were called *Ocean Hope 1, 2* and *3*. They were all crewed by unification members with experience in other parts of the country. Later, the fourth trawler, Green Hope, would come.

Few oceans could compare to Alaska's waters, which took many fishermen's lives every year. Six years later, one of those boats sank, coming back from the Bering Sea, taking all the crew into the dark, deep waters of the Gulf of Alaska during an incredible storm. Sixteen years later, another would sink – luckily, everyone survived that time.

Salmon season

Alaska is amazing and beautiful, wild and rugged, scattered with rivers that thaw in the summer and over one hundred million salmon return after living in the ocean for up to four years for some species. The

Alaskans come out of hibernation and the fishermen prepare for the harvest in the early summer after a cold winter. The whole economy comes to life with great anticipation for a good year.

Fishermen in small salmon seiners fish in the summer months. It used to be a profitable business, but now, with the glut of farm-raised salmon, fishermen's prices have sharply declined. In those good years between 1987 and 2000, a crew member could earn $40,000 for a few months of work.

Fishing was a family affair for many and the children of the fishermen were lucky as they received training as they grew up experiencing nature and learning to work hard. The Chinese were the first to work in the canneries in the early 1900s.

Now, a large population of Hispanic and Filipino workers has migrated to work in the canneries during the year and college kids come and work to raise money during summer break.

Father and Mother Moon and their 16-year-old son Heung Jin

Eugene, we never imagined Father and Mother Moon would come to Kodiak Island, but in August 1983, about three months after I arrived, they arrived and stayed at our small community three-bedroom company house.

There were only a handful of us living in Kodiak at the time. This was the first time for almost everyone to be in such an intimate setting with Father and Mother Moon. We felt like the disciples of Jesus as we sat and ate together in the living room.

We watched Father making his halibut rigs for the next day's fishing. Their sixteen-year-old son, Heung Jin Nim, also came with them. He was so respectful that we were all very impressed with him.

The next day, we flew in a floatplane to Shuyak Island, north of Kodiak.

Three islands make up the Kodiak archipelago and Shuyak is the northern island. We visited a local fisherman and his wife, who had a small cabin on the island. I don't believe anyone else lived on this remote island.

Red and his wife built their cabin in that wilderness. They were true Alaskans who fished and lived off the land.

Father Moon teaches his son Heung Jin how to prepare a tackle to catch halibut at the Bancroft House in Kodiak.

Father was so inspired to meet Red and Debbie and impressed with their lifestyle living off the land that he called this Redhead a real man of the wild. He even mentioned him and his wife in his Sunday service in New York.

That day, Father and Mother Moon and Heung Jin Nim went fishing in a twenty-eight-foot open boat and Red and Debbie took the rest of us fishing for halibut in their salmon seiner. Father caught his first halibut.

Years later, the couple were fishing for crab on the south end of Kodiak Island when the boat started taking on water and they were forced to abandon their boat and jump into the cold Alaskan waters in their survival suits.

Debbie had taken the Epirb, which gives off a signal that can be traced and a Coast Guard helicopter was dispatched to rescue them. In the dark of night, the helicopter was able to find her and a crewman holding her up in the rolling waves. Unfortunately, they weren't able to find Red. Like many other fishermen throughout the years, he was lost at sea.

The lives of Alaska fishermen were always at risk. They knew their lives could be lost at any time, making them more sensitive. They understood and felt the presence of another world as they guided their ships through the oceans. Living in a small community under those conditions made for a closer community. It did take years to melt the ice of the community towards us.

As there were no cell phones in those days, we communicated with fishing boats by single sideband radio.

I would call the boats in the early morning and late evening to schedule deliveries and sometimes, I would hear somebody yell out "Moonie, get off the radio!"

Father Moon and ISA managers are happy catching a halibut, 16 year old second son Heung Jin Nim, on the right. I am in the back without a hat.

The plant employees were mainly Filipino workers who would work eleven months of the year. Many of them would return to their families in the Philippines for a month in December.

We would later hear in December that year that Father Moon's son, Heung Jin Nim, was involved in a serious car accident. A truck had lost control and collided with his car. He died two days later, on January 2nd, 1984, in upstate New York. This incident was shocking for our church community.

I still remember the photos of Father and Mother Moon praying over his body, offering their child back to God. Heung Jin Nim Nim's accident occurred when Father Moon was speaking at a rally in Korea. The Communists had come to assassinate him and we were told that Heung Jin Nim became the offering to heaven for Father Moon's protection.

Kodiak became their second home

Little did we know that Father and Mother Moon would come to Kodiak at least twice a year in the succeeding years.

Father and Mother Moon fishing in calm waters.

In later years, Father said he regarded Kodiak as his second hometown. They came eighty-five times, spending long hours in the ocean and the rivers from early morning to late at night. Like the holy man who would go to the mountain, he would go to the ocean. He seemed to gain energy from the ocean and looked younger every day. Kodiak was a place where he would come to pray and meditate on the next events and projects.

His presence on the ocean was quiet as he seemed to commune with the universe. How could we understand this man who began his movement as the Holy Spirit Association for the Unification of World Christianity? He started evangelizing from a hut made from GI ration boxes in war-torn Korea and built a worldwide movement in a relatively short time. He had the heart to forgive all those that had maligned him throughout his life. This is where I learned the heart to forgive your enemy.

He was constantly thinking and praying about solving world problems and throwing out seeds, hoping that some would bear fruit and another opportunity would arise to create a better world. The organizations he had started and initiated for that dream to be realized involved every sector of society. Their lives were an incredible desire to end the suffering of humanity and the determination to change the course of human history.

The organizations were created to reach every level of society, from college students to scientists, professors, religious leaders and parliamentarians. The Women's Federation for World Peace was created in 1992 by Mother Moon to emphasize the role of women in a family, community, society and on the global path to peace.

The name of our movement was finally changed in 1994 to the Family Federation for World Peace and Unification. Sun Moon University in

South Korea educates students from around the world. Throughout the years, many new organizations have been created, like the American Clergy

Mother and Father Moon with a beautiful salmon caught in Buskin River in Kodiak.

Leadership Conference in 2000, the Inter Religious Federation for Peace in 2001, the Universal Peace Federation in 2005, the SunHak Peace Prize in 2015 to honor the late Father Moon, given to the most accomplished scientists, doctors and educators from around the world.

International Seafoods of Alaska

Our company processed salmon in the summer months and initially, only a few Kodiak fishermen would deliver fish to our plant because we were the new kids on the block.

To make it more challenging, we were the "Moonie" company, as the fishing industry called it. The fishermen had their customary plants to which they felt comfortable to deliver their catch. It took years to gain the local salmon fishermen's trust, so in the earlier years, we had to send our tender boats farther to procure our salmon from two other sources in Alaska – Chignik on the Aleutian chain and Egegik in Bristol Bay.

Our tender boats would buy salmon in Chignik from fishermen and ferry it back to Kodiak in refrigerated seawater to keep it fresh. The trip back to Kodiak was through the Shelikof Strait, notorious for its lousy weather. Those long and rough trips were hard on the fish quality, but we had to get fish from somewhere to keep our processing plant busy. The quality of the salmon, especially the salmon roe, would be affected by literally being in a washing machine on the way back.

The salmon season was hectic from June through September. The Alaskan days were long, with sunrise at 5:00 a.m. and it didn't get dark until after 11:00 p.m.

We purchased a buying station in Egegik in Bristol Bay and bought salmon from beach set net fishermen. Old WWII warplanes, DC6, DC3 and C119, were contracted before the season to fly the processed salmon iced and toted back to Kodiak, which was always a challenge because Kodiak was notorious for foggy weather conditions.

On bad weather days, getting an opening of good weather to land in Kodiak was always a challenge. I would call Winki, who managed his flight crews and made the decision to go for it if I saw a slight clearing of clouds. It would cost double the price if the plane couldn't land on the first attempt. Time was always a factor in keeping the fish fresh and getting the fish to processing as soon as possible.

For some years, I often slept in my office during the peak of the salmon season in Bristol Bay, to communicate with the beach operation, arrange for the flights for pickups and communicate with the tenders and fishing boats. The flight crews were brave because they had to land on a beach on low tide to be able to load and take off before the tide returned.

One night, a DC6 crashed on the beach at midnight during takeoff. Luckily, the crew survived with relatively minor injuries. 30,000 pounds of salmon was smoked as the plane caught fire and melted. This was the life of the Alaskan pilots and I believe most of those pilots lost their lives over the later years, either fighting bushfires or flying other dangerous missions.

One of the DC6 crews we were contracting one year went missing one morning and we later heard that they had made a trip in the night to California and were arrested for drug smuggling, so we lost that flight crew right in the middle of the season.

Living on Kodiak Island

I look back at the experience in Kodiak and wish it hadn't taken so long to get to know some of the fine people we would later learn to love. This was a small community of primarily fishermen and related industries and a large Coast Guard force living on an island in the Gulf of Alaska.

About 10,000 people were living on the Island then – half were members of the Coast Guard and their families. Kodiak Island has the most extensive Coast Guard base in America. We Unificationists, initially, were seen as outsiders belonging to a crazy cult in this small town and we were treated as such, unfortunately, for a long time.

I know how difficult it is to be discriminated against and how painful and lonely you can feel when you're not welcomed and accepted by others who see you as someone strange. My whole experience in the movement had been that way and now it was also on a business level. For many years, we would be ignored and shunned by some of the community. It took years to gain their trust.

First visit to New Zealand with my wife and Jin Joo

In December 1984, Jin Joo was eight months old when we went to New Zealand to introduce Izabela and their new granddaughter to the family. Izabela would arrive a few days before me as I had been on a business trip in Japan and happened to stay an extra day in Hawaii.

As I was flying into New Zealand that morning, my Scottish Grandmother died. She was over ninety and couldn't hold out any longer.

Holding Jin Joo and a silver salmon with our friend Umeno.

She passed into the spiritual world an hour before I arrived at my parent's home. I was happy that she could hold Jin Joo and meet

Izabela. She was a devout Christian who raised three children and played piano for her church for many years.

A few days after the funeral, as we were sitting together watching TV, my mother suddenly got up and said she smelled something. She rushed downstairs to where my grandmother had lived. A strong smell of incense was in my grandmother's room. My mother cried out for us to come downstairs.

We all hurried down and Izabela could also smell the scent, but my Dad and I couldn't smell anything. It was unusual for my mother to smell anything because, for years, a nose problem had blocked those senses.

She became a little hysterical and asked us if the priest had come by because it was the same incense used in the Catholic Church and Nanna wasn't Catholic. My Grandmother was with us in spirit.

A visit by a priest

My parents and family weren't happy that I had become a member of the Unification Church.

The heart of a good mother is always thinking about her children and over the years, while I was away in America, I would periodically telephone home.

My mother always said, "Martyn, it's time to return to New Zealand. You have had a good look around."

I have been fortunate to have parents who unconditionally loved me. That love, I believe, has helped me to understand the love of God.

My mother asked the Catholic priest to come to the house to talk and persuade me to leave the Unification Church.

I was surprised when he showed up at the door.

We greeted him and my mother said, "Father, please talk some sense into my son because he has joined the Moonie cult."

The priest said, "Do you know that you are following false beliefs? The Unification Church is misleading you."

I was scared, thinking this could be the beginning of my deprogramming.

Some parents who were unhappy to know their child was involved in the movement would hire deprogrammers, paying them as much as $25,000 to have their child abducted. In America, members were grabbed off the street by these criminals, thrown into a car to be taken and held against their will to break their faith.

This also happened in other countries, especially in Japan, where it wasn't classed as a criminal offense to abduct someone to break their faith like it was in America. In Japan, forty-three hundred members were taken against their will over the years and one was held for as long as twelve years but finally returned to the movement.

I had known members whom deprogrammers in America had abducted. Some left the movement after that experience and others returned.

I was worried and caught off guard by his sudden presence, expecting others to come and take me off somewhere for a deprogramming. I came out on the attack and asked him who he was to say I was misguided when the Catholic Church still taught about the Immaculate Conception and didn't allow priests to marry.

I told him how Father Moon had uncovered the mysteries of the Bible revealed in the Divine Principle and he would learn much if he read it. I tried to argue that Jesus had a physical father because God always works through universal laws.

But he responded, "Mrs. Byrne. I'm sorry, but I can't do anything with him. I am afraid he is brainwashed!" And stormed out the door.

I felt sorry for him as I watched him leave – a priest's life must be incredibly lonely. I believe in the future, the Catholic Church will allow its priests to marry, especially now as the church is declining worldwide. A man or woman responding to God's calling to be a priest needs a husband or wife to create a Godly family and be an example to other parishioners.

Returning to Alaska

We left New Zealand and flew with Jin Joo, heading back to Alaska, which I was still learning to love.

This had been my first trip back to New Zealand in seven years and I was happy to have met family and friends again after being away for so long. The summer had rejuvenated us and I still cherish the photos of Jin Joo, a little doll, looking so brown and healthy.

We stayed for a month before returning to Alaska in the dead of winter, a shock to the system. I immediately missed the summers in New Zealand and the joy of swimming at the beaches in the warm waters. The Alaskan waters were far more treacherous, only allowing a person approximately twenty minutes exposed in the ocean before succumbing to hypothermia and death.

Boston Whaler

It was the year before Jean, a French member, was injured in Chignik. He and I took a small boat, a Boston Whaler, to the North of Kodiak Island during the pink salmon season to visit a tender boat captain whom we had contracted to buy and transport salmon back to our processing plant.

It was getting dark and the weather turned ugly before returning home. We hadn't prepared well and weren't carrying any survival equipment. The Boston Whaler wasn't a good seaboat and breaking waves filled the boat.

The bilge pumps weren't working, so I instructed Jean to stay on his knees in the back of the boat and keep bucketing using a small can while we slogged home.

Happily, we arrived back in Kodiak town without incident.

Chignik on a three-wheeler

It must have been around 1986 when two of us flew on a charter flight to Chignik, a village on the Aleutian chain in Alaska. We were preparing for the salmon season and wanted to meet fishermen committed to fishing for our company that season.

We stayed at a fisherman's house and used his three-wheeler dirt bike to get around the village. Jean was driving and I was on the back as we headed up a hill and came to a light snowfall at the crest.

I said we should push the three-wheeler over the top and he said he would drive it through the snow. I decided to get off the back and Jean accelerated, tipping the bike backward. He called out that he had injured his back and lay on the ground groaning.

I didn't think he was seriously hurt and I said I could carry him down the hill. He said not to touch him and to go for help. I covered him with my jacket and ran for help.

A medevac charter flight took him to the Kodiak Hospital, where he nearly died. Later he was transferred to an Anchorage hospital to be treated for a severe spinal injury.

I might have been injured too, if I hadn't got off the back of the three-wheeler.

North Garden Residence

In the fall of 1986, our Kodiak congregation purchased land to build a house for Father and Mother Moon and all the guests who would come during the summer months. The design would have an Alaskan country aura. We would name it North Garden.

I was responsible for helping design and build North Garden, a three-story 10,000 square foot guest house, with the parameters that the Moon family would use half of the top floor area when they visited Kodiak. The rest of the house would be dedicated to accommodating and caring for the many guests who would come with them.

It became a team effort as the Korean leader, David, and I devised a plan. A local draftsman had great ideas to enhance the external design by enlarging the windows and changing the roof shape. A local engineer gave us the structural plans before David drew the plans for construction purposes. We made a few design changes as the house was being framed up. Luckily, I had played a lot of pool in my youth and realized that the pool room was too small, so we lost a few feet of the dining room as the wall was moved to widen the pool room.

With a budget of about $800,000, the project began by cutting and clearing trees from the land. The City of Kodiak allowed us to be the building contractor for the project.

I advertised for a lead carpenter and interviewed four prospects, deciding on the one with more framing experience. A framing package was ordered from Seattle and when it arrived about two weeks later, three more local carpenters were hired.

We began to build in the winter, with the deadline to be completed for the following summer of 1987. The electrical, concrete flat work and roofing were contracted to local subcontractors. Plumbing and heating were a question as we needed a licensed plumber to do the work.

I checked with the Department of Labor and Industries and they agreed to acknowledge my New Zealand plumbing license and grant me an Alaskan license if I passed the exam for a journeyman license. I passed the exam and hired a plumber by the hour. Later in the project, another plumber asked if we needed help. He was a gift from God.

We built through a rough winter. The concrete foundations had to be covered and heated with propane heaters to prevent them from cracking from the cold as they were curing. I hired a mason from Anchorage on the mainland to build a beautiful fireplace that was the living room's centerpiece. Mr. Chai and Steven went to Seattle and purchased all the interior furnishings for the house. Carpets, doors, tiles, cabinets, plumbing fixtures, trim, etc., were soon on their way to Kodiak by container barge.

North Garden residence opened its doors in 1987.

It had been a hard push through the winter to complete North Garden before guests arrived in the summer of 1987.

The bulldozer was quickly moved to the back of the house as the guests were coming from the airport. The carpenters went out the back door with their tools as the guests entered the front door.

One hundred and fifty Korean professors arrived with Father and Mother Moon. These professors had to be accommodated and fed and I still remember being worried that they would spill and stain the new light green carpet with kimchi juice.

That evening, the house was packed with the professors in sleeping bags all over the house. Preparing them to go fishing, some on the boats and some on the river, was challenging for the staff.

It was quite a sight for the locals to see the whole line of people on the riverbanks in yellow rain gear trying to catch their first salmon.

Father Moon in my old pickup truck

My old Ford pickup truck had one bench seat and a three-speed manual column shift on the steering column.

In those days, we didn't have cell phones to communicate with our twenty-eight-foot sports boats and communicated by marine radio. The radio in my office was set on a matching channel with the boats.

It was usual for Father Moon to come back late, except for this particular day when they returned earlier. I either missed or didn't receive a call on the radio that they were on the way back and there wasn't a car ready to take them back to the North Garden house.

Mr. Choi, the company's president, ran up to my office and asked for the keys to my truck. He was going to drive Father Moon back to the house.

After he rushed out the door, I realized he wouldn't know how to drive a manual transmission vehicle, so I ran down the stairs through the front door into the street to see Mr. Choi and Father Moon sitting in the truck. I was right – Mr. Choi didn't know how to drive a manual shift.

The truck was lurching and jerking down the road as he had let the clutch out too fast.

I ran beside the truck and told Mr. Choi to get on the truck bed. Anyone else seeing what happened would have enjoyed the comedy, but I jumped into the driver's seat, mortified that I didn't have the car ready and now here sat Father in the passenger seat of my old truck. I'm a perfectionist in preparation, so this was a challenge to take lightly.

Still, Father didn't seem upset about the incident and probably enjoyed a different experience. He was quiet as we drove back to the house.

There was a time when they had just landed in Kodiak and I was driving Father and Mother Moon from the Kodiak airport. He asked me if the salmon were running in the Buskin River yet and I said I was not sure and he said to drive down to check the river. It was a little early in the season and we didn't see any fish in the river.

Fishing with Father on the trawler Ocean Hope 2

In 1989, about twenty of us accompanied Father Moon on a fishing trawler for a day.

It was summer and the weather was spectacular. Father Moon directed the captain to wait and keep fishing before pulling the net in.

The net was packed with fish when we finally retrieved it.

I am standing in the front on the right of Father Moon, with my hands in the air.

We all gathered, standing on the bag of fish for a photo, all of us happy to be together with Father Moon reminding us of Jesus helping Peter to get a big catch.

Building the first church and a training center

In 1989, our community decided to build a church next to North Garden guesthouse.

Several building lots had been bought in 1986, big enough to accommodate North Garden and a church. I was again responsible for helping design and build the church. As this was a public building, the city classed it as commercial, so the project was more complicated than North Garden.

David and I worked on the plans. The church leader, Mr. Choi, was also very involved. The community also gave a lot of input. We decided the church would be on the top floor and a daycare facility downstairs. Most of the families involved in the business were having children. We sought the help of a structural engineer and David drew up the plans.

We were lucky to employ the same lead carpenter we hired for North Garden because he was easy to work with and we worked well together. Three additional carpenters were hired and we started building. The basic framing structure stood as Father drove into North Garden in the summer of 1989.

Looking at the building, he said it was too small and asked us to build it twice as big. I admit I was shocked, but not as much as my carpenter crew when I told them about a change. When I told them we had to build it twice as big, they thought I was joking. We went to the drawing table and made it twice as big.

The addition included a commercial kitchen and dining room upstairs, men's and women's bathrooms with showers, plus two large hot tubs adjoining each bathroom on the ground floor to warm up cold bodies after coming from a day of fishing.

The church was completed in 1990. It was the first church building we built in America. We called it Angel Garden and in December of that year, we had a beautiful Opening Ceremony.

HSA-UWC Angel Garden and Training Center Opening Dec 1990.

The exemplary lives of Father and Mother Moon

It wasn't a concept but a reality as Father and Mother Moon showed a deep reverence for God in everything they did. The whole community witnessed how a man and woman together can live a life dedicated to

God and sacrifice for a world that had scorned them, even though they had poured out their hearts with concern for everyone. All of us captured the heart of goodness through the examples of their saintly lives.

When Jin Joo Ellen was older, she would come to help Izabela serve Father and Mother Moon and the guests at breakfast. I was so proud of her as she was learning to serve others. It was a vital lesson.

She was there when Father talked about the importance of sexual purity, which was his favorite topic. He spoke many times quite graphically about the importance and holiness of sexual organs. He would stress that the sexual organ does not exist for yourself but only for your spouse and should never be shared with anybody else but your one true love. The sexual act between a husband and his wife is a beautiful encounter where God rejoices and allows his love to participate in the procreation process.

The womb should be a holy, sacred place where the child will start to develop. Women must realize that their bodies are created for maternity's sake and should not be obscenely displayed for everyone to see.

At one breakfast, he explained how God had created the world. Before it unfolded through millions of years, there was a design, a blueprint first and men and women were to be at the core of his creation. He explained the purpose behind all the creation. He loved to talk about the eyes and how they were created to see, how the eyelashes were designed to protect them from wind, dust, or rain and how the eyebrows were to collect the sweat coming from the forehead. Everything was created with a purpose.

Izabela and our girls checking out the salmon catch.

Jin Joo heard some of these talks and was inspired early on to find true love in her own life. She had a strong passion and dedication to pure love and the ideal of a true family. That teaching helped her to join Pure Love Alliance rallies and tours later in life.

Father Moon inspects the Angel Garden

In 1990, our new church building was completed.

Father walked over from North Garden to the sanctuary that summer and a small group of us followed.

He began talking and we sat on the hard industrial carpeting because no chairs were set up. Many of us hadn't sat cross-legged since we joined the movement years before. In the oriental tradition, sitting with your feet stretched out in front of you is bad manners.

Father was amused to see us struggling to be comfortable and told us we should exercise daily. He joked with a few heavy brothers and said they were too fat and they shouldn't overeat and eat like a bird – a bit of everything.

He then surprised us by showing us some of his exercises. We were amazed to see him bend and touch his chin to his knees and lift his leg behind his neck with incredible flexibility for a man over seventy. He certainly put us all to shame. He said he exercised every morning. With his busy schedule, I couldn't imagine how he found the time.

It wasn't until I reached the same age that I could fully appreciate that experience and realize how difficult it is to exercise the body at an older age. I had read that he had exercised and washed his body every day with a small rag dipped in water when in the communist labor camp. He must have trained his body over many years to reach that level of flexibility.

That experience inspired me to start exercising, doing yoga and Tai chi every day in my older years, another way he taught me to improve myself.

Hunting on Kodiak Island

The men in our community would have a yearly hunting competition.

We would use one of the sister company trawlers to sleep on and they provided a great cook. Zola had escaped communist rule in the People's Republic of Hungary years earlier and joined the movement. He looked after us tired and hungry hunters, so we were always comfortable and had plenty to eat.

There was better hunting on the west side of Kodiak Island and we hunted in pairs. We took a boat to shore to spend the day hunting, looking for the trophy rack that could win us a new rifle if we won. Other prizes were for the taking too.

Neil and I would fly to Anchorage to buy a collection of guns and knives as prizes for the competition. Most of the friends I knew in Alaska had a weapon and it was common to see a rifle hanging in the back window of pickup trucks. We had never heard of a mass shooting in those days. Everyone was cautious with their weapons.

That year, the weather turned nasty when we were hunting. Returning to the skiff in the late afternoon, we found the outboard engine wouldn't start. White caps formed in the bay and returning to the trawler would be dangerous.

We took turns trying to pull start the outboard engine without any luck. We found ourselves stranded on the beach. The wind was howling and the weather turned bitterly cold. With nowhere to hide from the weather, we rounded up driftwood, built a fire on the beach and got as close as possible without catching our clothes on fire.

I was wearing cotton clothing, which I decided would not be worn again while hunting in Alaska. If it weren't for matches somebody had produced, we wouldn't have been able to build a fire that we stoked all night to keep us alive until the morning. Without that fire, I would have had hypothermia and wouldn't have made it through to morning.

In the morning, the weather had settled and the engine came to life on the first try.

As we were heading from the shore, I thought the engine not starting the night before may have saved our lives.

Kodiak Hunting and Fishing Competition: 2 1/2-year-old Jin Joo with her mother on the lower far right. Jin Joo is looking at me at the top very left.

Training Leaders

Father and Mother Moon rarely came to Kodiak alone. Many church leaders were usually invited to experience the beauty of Alaska and spend intimate time with them.

Father would spend many hours teaching, guiding and uplifting these leaders. Through fishing, he wanted to teach them to cultivate patience and a spirit to overcome hardships, toughen them up and spend time with him so that they could understand his heart.

Kodiak is a glorious place when the weather is fine, but unfortunately, this is a rare occasion.

Most days fishing around Kodiak are bitterly cold in the ocean, making it a perfect place to be uncomfortable. The schedule was demanding and the conditions were worse.

Leaders, mainly Koreans, Japanese and Americans, were invited as it was the perfect place for training. Fishing in Kodiak was no picnic. It was an ideal place to give them a break from their responsibilities. Most importantly, fishing was a great way of helping to unite the leaders. It is not easy to have people from different nations working together, so it has been an enormous hurdle and handicap for our movement because of language and cultural differences, a challenge of epic proportions.

Still, through the challenge, we all have gained and learned a great deal about each other's cultures and much will be passed on to the next generation. People from different nations fishing together on a small open boat in cold and inclement weather with a demanding schedule and conditions was an experience they would never forget. They fished in open twenty-eight-foot boats for halibut and salmon on the ocean and fished the rivers for salmon when it was too dangerous for ocean fishing.

The North Garden guesthouse in Kodiak had a large open living room with a beautiful stone fireplace as the center and a long rectangular dining table that could seat about twenty people.

Father sometimes spoke for hours to all who shared in the breakfast meal before they went fishing and when they came back for dinner, many times late into the evening.

There were times during those years when I sat at the breakfast and dinner table. I felt uncomfortable because I thought about all the religious leaders of the different denominations who should have been there in my place to attend such a profound Teacher, Visionary and Messiah. I felt like one of the disciples sitting with Jesus, trying to understand someone as vast as the universe.

Father and Mother Moon with a salmon catch. I am the tallest guy in the back.

Father and Mother seemed so ordinary at times, especially when his beautiful smile and laughter would light up the room. They were such precious times to see them together.

Father and Mother Moon were never late to greet God at 5:00 a.m. every Sunday. This had always been their tradition, I would expect, throughout their lives together since their Blessing of Marriage in 1960.

Church members and guests would join the service in the North Garden living room. Father would speak to everyone gathered close and sitting on the floor.

We were very fortunate to have had such an intimate experience where most church members worldwide had no opportunity like that and never shared such a close experience with Father and Mother Moon.

Working with Father Moon

I helped with general affairs for some years when Father and Mother Moon came to Kodiak. My job was to make sure their visits went smoothly. If something was needed, I made sure it happened.

Sometimes, we had a schedule for the day, but Father would change it at the last moment, possibly to keep us on our toes. Like life itself, surprises always come. I was fortunate to see their lifestyle up close and personal.

Father seemed to go out of his way to be uncomfortable. Kodiak is the place to arrange that because of its rugged weather and treacherous waters. He fished from a twenty-eight-foot open boat that didn't have a toilet for many of the years he came.

The media portrayed him as a wealthy businessman, but a twenty-eight-foot open boat is far from luxurious. There is nowhere to hide from the brutal Alaskan weather and he would sit in the back of the boat exposed to the weather all day.

He must have trained his body to withstand all the harsh conditions during the six times he was imprisoned and tortured throughout his life.

Preparing all the gear for fishing. Father Moon and I are watching.

Kodiak's weather wasn't a match for the seacoast of Hungnam, where he served two years and eight months of hard labor before being liberated by the UN bombardment of the labor camp. He told us how the winter wind was as painful as a knife as it cut into their naked bodies when they were stripped while guards searched them each morning for contraband items.

He went out fishing in Kodiak even on the gnarly days when few fishermen would brave the conditions, many days returning to the dock in the dark of night.

Father Moon returning from halibut fishing.

We had a small floating dock big enough for a few boats to tie up with a steep set of stairs up to a concrete driveway where I'd park the car with the engine on and heat turned up – probably too hot for anyone coming in from the cold, but he never complained. I could see he was exhausted as he pulled himself into the car after being in the weather all day.

The ride back to the house was silent as he sat beside me in the front seat. Even though I had driven him a number of times, I was always nervous sitting next to this great man, the Messiah. I wondered what he was thinking about as we drove back to North Garden. I felt inadequate, as I suppose the disciples of Jesus must have felt, unable to understand that this was indeed a man of God.

I witnessed for years that even though he must have been tired, he kept talking and teaching even minutes before he would depart for the airport to fly out of Kodiak. For most of my years in Kodiak, he traveled by commercial airlines.

We would all go with our families to the airport terminal to bid them farewell. We all felt an empty longing as we watched their plane lift over the bay on their way to a stopover in Anchorage.

Forty-three Japanese members

In 1990, after completing the church project, I returned to my position as plant manager, for which I had been responsible since 1985.

Someone else had taken up my position when I managed the building of North Garden and the church. The company had hired a day and a night shift of over one hundred workers on each shift. Large volumes of fish would be delivered daily and it wasn't unusual to see a million pounds of pollock delivered in a day to be processed into filets for the U.S. market.

In 1984, forty-three young Japanese women who were members matched to American husbands and were Blessed in Marriage at the same ceremony in New York arrived to work at our plant in Kodiak. The plan was to train them to start fish businesses in different parts of the world.

They were amazing. I quickly realized how diligent, reliable, united and intelligent the Japanese people are. Quickly, they organized themselves to work in processing the different fish species. The plant was cold and wet, but they still came to work every day. Many became the line leaders in the various processing areas.

Izabela trained a few of them to help with fish quality inspection, as we already had three children and she could not be at work every day.

They left Kodiak in 1989 to join their husbands and start their own families. They had sacrificed their lives to come and work in Kodiak and when they departed, there was a huge void to fill, not only in the fish plant but also in helping with the many guests who came to Kodiak with Father and Mother Moon. The managers' wives did most of the domestic work, including cooking, cleaning and serving.

Father Moon talking to the Japanese women and others at North Garden.

A new challenge

After the Japanese women left Kodiak, we had to hire and build a new team of processors who, understandably, were more challenging to manage.

I took the position of Plant Manager too seriously, spending many hours every day trying to build a successful company. Those were long, hard days as I was responsible for over 200 people with a day and a night shift. The fishing industry was quickly changing. Every company in Alaska aimed to process more fish daily. New machinery was required and processing lines were constantly changed and upgraded to accomplish this goal most efficiently.

This experience in Alaska gave me an excellent chance to work with people from many nationalities. There, I learned to respect other cultures and traditions different from mine.

My experience as a plant manager was invaluable in many ways. I learned to work with others, listen to their opinions and consider their feelings. I knew that sometimes I had to make tough decisions and leadership is lonely.

Having at least one person to support you in that role is precious. I felt God sent such a person to help, a Greek, whose name was Costas. He came to work at the plant without a penny to his name. I could see he was down on his luck, so I gave him a job, initially cleaning up and organizing the metal yard of scrap and processing tables and equipment.

I later discovered he had been made bankrupt. He had owned two restaurants in Kodiak. His first restaurant was doing so well that he opened another. Unfortunately, he lost the lease for the first, affecting the second restaurant, which still needed to be solvent.

He was drinking heavily at night and smoking three packs a day, trying to recover from his loss when he came looking for a job. He told me later that the police stopped him for the third time for drinking and driving and on the way to the police station, he pleaded with the policeman to give him another chance, saying he would give up drinking that night. The policeman had a soft heart and second thoughts and stopped the car, telling Costas he had another chance.

Costas never drank again. He soon went to Greece and found a wife, bringing her back to cold Alaska.

I soon realized that he was intelligent, hard working and, most importantly, he liked and respected people. Eventually, I promoted him to production manager. He understood a dollar and learned how to increase production and decrease labor costs. We worked closely together to build a processing team and are still friends.

Most valuable was the understanding that culture does start at the top. As a leader, I saw how my culture and vision, or my concerns, if conveyed and stressed correctly, were disseminated to all who worked in the plant. This was an important lesson to understand. Authentic leadership is not only management but also implementing the vision.

Having had the experience of managing a company, I thought about Father Moon and witnessed how he created a movement that included people from every culture, race and religion.

Fishing on Kenai River

In 1991, Father and Mother Moon returned to Kodiak. We expected it would be regular fishing around Kodiak. At the last minute, they decided to go fishing on the Kenai Peninsula on the mainland of Alaska, where some of the biggest king salmon are caught.

I arranged two private planes to fly fifteen Japanese church leaders to meet Father in Kenai. Others had traveled directly to Kenai from Anchorage. I went with them to the Kodiak airport to ensure everything went as scheduled. I was concerned because we still hadn't arranged accommodation and logistics for the stay in Kenai due to the change of plans.

I helped load everyone onto the last plane with a worried heart that it could turn into custard with little support in Kenai. Before the doors closed on the charter, I thought I should go and help. As there was an extra seat, I jumped on board without any extra clothes or anything for the trip.

Arriving in Kenai, I was responsible for organizing accommodations and finding a charter boat to take everyone fishing the next day on the Kenai River, the longest river in Alaska. This was the peak of the season. Fishing charters and accommodations were all booked well before the season, so I had to find a place with vacancies and someone who was under-booked to take them fishing.

I usually did Logistics in Kodiak, so I knew the territory there. The mainland was a different story. All I could do was have faith in God, knowing everything would work out. I decided to water fast for three days to be as focused and create miracles because the circumstances were bleak to find accommodations for a large group. Luckily, we found places for everyone to stay a little out of town at a location different from Father and Mother Moon.

I called all the listed charter boat operators, as having a guide to fish the Kenai River for king salmon was mandatory. Fishing for salmon in the Kenai meant you floated down the river by boat, casting as you went. We found a charter for Father and a few leaders. The others fished from the side of the river. We were all happy to experience Father returning that afternoon with a seventy-two pound king salmon, a huge fish.

I arranged an early breakfast of bacon and eggs for twenty-one Japanese leaders the following day. I asked the cook to have everything prepared by 6:00 a.m. That morning, they received a call to come directly to the hotel where Father and Mother Moon were staying at 5:00 a.m.

It was very humorous as they filed down the stairs and loaded up into vans as the cook came out saying the food was nearly ready. I told him I would return and pay him as we drove away.

As I looked back, he was staring in disbelief, watching us drive away while he held his spatula in the air.

Father and Mother Moon with close staff. I am in the back. Mr. Chai's son eldest son holding a King Salmon- a beautiful trophy.

Flying to Dutch Harbor Alaska

The fishing trip was over and we drove from Kenai back to Anchorage for our flight back to Kodiak.

As we waited in the Anchorage airport for the plane to Kodiak, Father said he wanted to go to Dutch Harbor, the center of Alaska's crab and bottom fishing industry.

The documentary series *Deadliest Catch* shows the life of the king crab fishermen. It's an unbelievable battle against the elements to catch crab in the harshest weather imaginable. Only five of us were there because the others had left for Japan that morning.

I quickly made reservations on the commuter plane to Dutch Harbor on the Alaskan Peninsula.

Arriving in Dutch Harbor, Father and Mother Moon walked up the tallest hill closest to the airport. We followed. There, overlooking Unalaska Bay, he prayed for lost fishermen, including Jack White, a member from Kodiak who had died at sea with three other crew members in 1989 when their trawler, the *Ocean Hope 2*, sank on its way to shelter from fifty-mile-an-hour winds and freezing conditions.

I was amazed that Father Moon would remember Jack's name in his prayer and as he prayed in Korean, I distinctly heard him say the name of Jack White.

Jack was an excellent pool player. I asked him where he learned to play so well.

He was raised by his grandparents, who owned a bar and pool hall. That explained why he beat me most of the time.

I wondered if the *Ocean Hope 2* was doomed after being outfitted for fishing in the Bering Sea.

As they were leaving town, Jack cut the corner too sharply on the buoy in Kodiak and hit a rock, tearing open the hull. As water rushed in, he turned the boat around and steamed as fast as the boat would go to the fuel dock just down the channel, where he knew they had pumps to keep afloat while a temporary patch could be installed to save the boat from sinking in the channel. The boat was repaired over a few weeks and left again to fish in the Bering Sea. Maybe it was a sign that he shouldn't have gone. He left behind his wife and small son.

We were given a tour of one of the biggest fish processing companies in Dutch Harbor.

Outside on the dock, as we were walking, one of the workers saw that we were taking a video, dropped his pants and showed his butt to Father and Mother Moon.

I was thinking about throwing him into the water, but Father and Mother Moon acted as if they didn't notice.

I felt that this symbolized what they had to endure every day. They lived a life of integrity in a world that often showed the opposite.

We hired a taxi to tour Dutch Harbor. The cab was dirty both outside and inside. There was dust over all the seats. I was ashamed that I didn't have a cleaner vehicle for them. Dutch Harbor is way out at the end of the Alaskan Peninsula and the heart of the fishing business in the U.S. Incredible volumes of fish are caught and harvested there – the most dangerous fishing in the world and the biggest crab and bottom fishery worldwide.

I thought about their lives as we traveled around Dutch Harbor in the old dusty cab. Father had started his first church made with cardboard boxes. He and Mother Moon had lived difficult lives but seemed as comfortable in an old beat-up van as in a brand-new vehicle. I was sitting next to Mother. I sat halfway on the chair to give her more space. She motioned me to move closer to her to be more comfortable.

At the airport, she called me into the gift store and bought a sweatshirt for me, which I treasured for many years.

I also had close experience fishing with her on the Russian River in Kodiak. I used a purple fishing fly that day and the silver salmon loved it. I was hooking up and passing the rod to Mother, who would reel in the fish. We went arm in arm to the other side of the river where the fish were more plentiful.

Meeting Gorbachev

In 1990, Father and Mother Moon organized a meeting of government and media in Moscow. This fulfilled their pledge in 1973 that one day, they would organize a "great rally for God in Moscow."

Father and Mother Moon met with President Mikhail Gorbachev during this conference, which coincided with their thirtieth wedding anniversary. Through several interviews, televised and in print, they gave a message of hope to the Soviet people, urging them to turn toward God. Father Moon told Gorbachev that the only way for the Soviet Union to survive was to continue his economic and political reforms and to allow freedom of religion.

Friendly meeting in Kremlin: Father and Mother Moon with Mikhail Gorbachev.

A meeting with Kim Il Sung

In December 1991, Father and Mother Moon risked their lives to travel to North Korea to meet with President Kim Il Sung. A Soviet-trained leader, under his regime Father Moon was arrested, tortured and sentenced to five years in Hungnam labor camp.

This trip for reconciliation was another example of forgiveness we learned through their lives. They went to North Korea to forgive and embrace Kim Il Sung, who had caused such misery for the Korean people and the world and themselves, not knowing if they would be allowed to leave North Korea after their meetings.

They always believed that uniting North and South Korea was essential in establishing world peace. The visit was a crucial meeting

Meeting of two leaders with opposing ideologies.

between a religious leader strongly opposing godless Juche ideology and Kim Il Sung, a ruthless leader suppressing any kind of religion or opposition in North Korea.

It had been more than forty years since they had been able to return to their hometowns. During their visit to North Korea, Father Moon was allowed to visit the house of his place of birth and put flowers on his parent's graves. He was tearfully welcomed with joy by his surviving relatives.

Built my house in Kodiak

After Jin Joo was born, we moved into an apartment complex, starting in a one-bedroom and moving to a bigger apartment as our family grew. When we were expecting our fourth child, the landlord told us we had to move because four children weren't allowed in the complex.

We started to think about building our own house. After completing North Garden and the Church with the daycare Angel Garden, I felt I could now build my own house.

With money from selling my house in New Zealand and Izabela's small inheritance from selling her parent's house, we could buy a building lot and, with bank financing, move forward to build our own house near Monashka Bay in Kodiak.

We had a contractor frame the house and I did the interior with some help from time to time. It wasn't easy working after hours and I remember crawling under the house at 11:00 p.m. in the cold of the winter installing plumbing and heating piping.

We had a beautiful home overlooking the Bay when our son was born.

Meeting in Auckland

In 1992 our family, already having three girls and a son, went to New Zealand in the winter when fishing was closed and the plant was doing the necessary maintenance for the following year.

1992 Summer Family Portrait.

    Izabela was often sick in Kodiak, coughing a lot and having asthma attacks and I thought the weather in New Zealand would be better for her health as it was summertime there.

    Eugene, we flew from Anchorage to Honolulu and stayed for a few days. Seeing my children getting on an escalator at the airport for the first time was a joy and I realized they would learn and experience many new things on this trip. It was their first real summer. To top it off, I rented a red convertible so these few days in Waikiki would never be forgotten. Swimming with tropical fish in Hanauma Bay's clear, warm waters was a real treat.

We were planning to stay in New Zealand and live close to my parents, family and friends. Somehow that plan changed very unexpectedly.

Our arrival in Auckland coincided with Father Moon's speaking tour. A friend called and told us that Father Moon was in Auckland and would be speaking the next day.

I immediately called the church center and asked how I could help. I was informed to come to the hotel on the fifth floor.

Arriving at the hotel and coming out of the elevator on the fifth floor, a door opened in front of me as I walked down the corridor and out came Won Joo McDevitt, a long-time assistant of Father and Mother Moon. We knew each other from Kodiak and were surprised to see each other.

I told her we were here in New Zealand visiting family.

She said to wait a minute and went back inside. She came out quickly and invited me in. I was surprised to see Father sitting with four other leaders at the table.

Father greeted me by saying, "Oh, you have come from Alaska."

I was invited to sit down. Then, a discussion started in Korean.

Soon, Peter Kim, one of Father Moon's associates, said, "The New Zealand leader would like you to stay in New Zealand and Mr. Park from Alaska would like you to return to Kodiak."

Then Father asked me, "What do you want to do?"

I was surprised that he would give me a choice. I knew that I quickly had the decision of my life to make. A flash of thoughts came to mind and my heart was calling me to stay in New Zealand as I thought about the warm beaches and the chance to join my New Zealand family again.

I had missed my parents, brothers and friends over the years and I wanted my children to experience Kiwi-style living where we could go to the beach together. But I also thought of Alaska and all that still had to be accomplished. I felt it was my mission and I couldn't leave Kodiak's business without bringing some success.

Father had talked so much throughout the years about peace coming to humanity in the future and the food problem would become the most serious issue for the world to solve. Produce from the land alone couldn't solve the food problem. Harvest from the land had to be complemented with seafood resources.

So, thinking about all those plans, I said, "Father, I think I should return to Alaska."

He said okay and that was it. The meeting quickly finished and I was soon returning to Alaska.

My family stayed in New Zealand for three months and lived on a small farm with my parents and one of my brothers. Izabela regained her health.

I am glad that Jin Joo, who was already nine, and the three other children experienced that time with their New Zealand family. The mosquitoes loved Jin Joo's blood and her face and legs were badly bitten during their stay.

Eugene, there are times when we have to make decisions in life that aren't always what we want. We just have to do what we know is the right thing at the time, even though it will require a certain amount of personal sacrifice. If we can follow that inner voice, life will always work out for the best. I have always tried to listen to that small, quiet voice and have found that following it has always led me in the right direction.

Father Moon often gave people choices. Other times, he gave direct orders for their lives because he could predict what would happen if they did it their way.

The goal of ten million pounds of pink salmon

In 1996, before the salmon season, we decided that our goal would be to buy ten million pounds of pink salmon from the salmon fishermen around Kodiak Island, much more than in previous years. We contracted with several larger tender boats to ferry the purchased salmon in refrigerated seawater to our processing facility.

All the Alaska companies that could process large volumes of pink salmon had canning lines. Our plant instead processed and froze the salmon, which was a much slower production.

Father and Mother Moon came to Kodiak before the pink salmon season. They were never involved in the day-to-day business, but at this particular breakfast, it was mentioned that we planned to buy ten million pounds of pink salmon that year. Father seemed happy to hear that the company was going for bigger goals and he gave a thumbs up.

I was concerned and felt more accountable to fulfill the season's goal because Father would possibly ask if we reached our goal after the season.

We soon found that the season produced a considerable return of pink salmon throughout Alaska. About one hundred million pink salmon are harvested in Alaska every year. I was then concerned about sales because if our frozen pink salmon didn't sell quickly, it would end up in cold storage. We would have to pay monthly storage fees.

We didn't have the financial capital to hold millions of pounds of salmon waiting for a sale. As it was a banner year, I was worried the selling price could drop because of supply and demand and we would eventually lose money. The cost of fish plus the processing fee, shipping and cold storage could be more than the final sale price. I was in a dilemma whether to follow my gut feeling and stop buying or continue to purchase fish. If we stopped buying salmon, we would have angry fishermen and Father gave us the green light to buy ten million pounds.

I knew we had sales for seven million pounds, so I decided to stop buying once we reached seven million pounds. We had angry fishermen and a few people who said I had no faith, but I had to follow my gut instincts. I was anxious that Father would eventually hear that I was responsible for not making the goal. Still, my take on it was although Father was happy to see us increasing processing volumes, he didn't understand the intricacies of the business and it was my decision based on experience.

It turned out that the price of pink salmon continued to drop as companies couldn't find enough buyers, finally selling and losing money.

I have always felt that we were free to do our best in every situation in the church. Some members thought Father was all knowing, but I believed he relied on us to make many daily decisions.

Transferring to Seattle

In 1995, I received a new position as a sales manager for our company. Our previous salespeople had left our company to start their own businesses, so I volunteered to take over their positions.

It was a challenging year for all of us as I had to rush down to Seattle to take over the sales for the company, leaving Izabela alone to look after the children and prepare to leave Kodiak.

Besides keeping her part-time job and training others, she was busy driving the kids to different activities like swimming, ballet, piano lessons, etc. One year before leaving, she started home schooling for our two oldest daughters in the first year of Middle School and third grade of Elementary school. It took her some time to understand the Alaskan curriculum. Our two younger children attended public school.

She always believed home education would be a safer environment and help develop parent-child relationships. She could not do this earlier because of her duties at the plant.

Izabela and the children were happy, preparing to leave Kodiak. Even Father Moon had called it "a prison without walls," describing the cold, wet and windy climate in the small Kodiak town.

When we finally arrived in Seattle at the end of August 1996, our daughter Jin Joo was twelve and the younger ones were nine and eight. Our youngest, the only boy, was six.

After spending a few months in Seattle before my family moved there, I realized I missed working at the plant, which I always found exciting, with many daily challenges. I found the sales job less interesting as I sat in the office in Seattle selling fish over the phone.

I returned to Kodiak to prepare to move out of Kodiak. I understood the Alaskan business well by this time, so it helped my work in the sales department. With an understanding of production and sales, I would decide what products to produce in Alaska. My only sales experience had been in flower and picture sales on the streets of New York many years before.

With nobody to train me in sales and explain how to price the products I sold, I quickly learned that supply and demand affected the sale price. I had worked close to the ocean as a plant manager for ten years, responsible for a processing plant with over 200 employees.

I missed all the action of the processing plant, the stress of managing all that would go on every day in an environment that was tough and, many times, chaotic. After living in Alaska for twelve years, it was quite an adjustment to live in a big city again and be in an office most of the day selling fish over the phone.

Three years later, the company's CEO decided to leave the company. As I had worked closely with him in Seattle, he recommended that I take his position in December 1998.

This proved to be a challenging experience for me.

Jin Joo leaves Seattle for a program in Korea

Before the new school year started in Seattle, we found a comfortable home to rent within walking distance of Greenwood Elementary School.

Our whole family had to adjust to life in a big city and new surroundings.

Also that year, Jin Joo was accepted to attend a one-year middle school program for foreigners in Korea to learn the language and get to know the country, its customs and traditions. She spent less than a month with us before leaving. About forty other students from different countries were with her in Seoul, South Korea. In the first days after arrival, playing ball on uneven surfaces, she broke a bone in her foot, which required a cast and walking with crutches. This condition affected her studies and daily living.

In November of that year, Izabela and our other daughter went to Korea to visit her and attend a spiritual revival. They noticed that Jin Joo had lost weight and was weak.

A few weeks later, we received a message that she had become frail and was not able to participate in any of the classes. Growing up, she had always been healthy and being unwell was unusual. She hoped to continue schooling there, but we had to bring her home.

After her health improved, she wanted to return, but we persuaded her there would be another opportunity later in her life.

Talent contest

Jin Joo's real passions were playing piano and ballet. She began private piano lessons when she was eight.

Being an impossible romantic and a dreamer, playing the piano suited her as she began to play the beautiful tunes that most budding pianists learn when they start.

When she returned from Korea, she played piano in our church Christmas Party talent competition. She felt unprepared to enter as she hadn't played for over six months.

I told her not to worry about technique but to "play from her heart."

She played so beautifully that she won first place. Her heart shone through the music.

Buying a 300 foot processing ship

In 1998, the CEO of our sister fishing company told me that a ninety-meter fishing factory ship, called a catcher processor in the industry, was for sale. The company that owned it had gone bankrupt and was selling the boat. He invited a few people to partner in a new venture he was putting together.

As a group, we could buy it if there were enough partners to invest and become percentage owners based on our investment. I raised money through a loan on the equity in our home. We decided to remain connected to the church business while managing the new enterprise.

After a short time, I realized it would be a conflict of interest to be involved in the new factory boat venture. The biggest concern for Izabela and myself was that we didn't want Father Moon to feel that I hadn't fulfilled my promise to him during our meeting in New Zealand, which was that I would return to Kodiak and manage the business.

With those thoughts, we decided as a family to pull out of the venture and determined to focus on the Kodiak and Seattle business.

I had always wanted to work with boats. It was an exciting chance to be involved and, hopefully, make more money, but we decided to terminate our involvement.

Dear Izabela, Martin and Sonia   Sun., Aug 31, 2002

I cannot speak the words to say how I grieve for all of you right now. What a bright candle Jin Joo was for this world!

She appreciated the beatiful in life. As her piano teacher, I saw how hard she would work to demonstrate that beauty in her playing. But I also learned so much about how profound she was in her thoughts about life, about the world, about her relationship with others.

I have had so many moments the last few days where I' ver become teary-eyed- particularly when I heard some beautiful music and I thought of how Jinn Joo would have appreciated it; or when I read something I thought of how she might reflect on it.

I just cannot get over the fact that this wonderful young woman has been stolen from us. The world NEEDS people like her to help us get on track and set our priorities straight.

Jin Joo had the capacity to jolt even me-and I am fairly strongly opinionated.

So rarely do you find a person her age so highly developed in ethical principles, societal views, caring for the world and loving the beautiful – not the materialistic part of life. I admired her so much. I also could see how close your family was and I knew that this lovely, lovely young girl did not develop in a vacuum. All of you help her to become what she was and she was so obviously grateful for what all of you contributed to her life. I know she continues to live in many, many hearts including my own. I hope all of you continue to feel her presence, her love, her beauty in your lives and that she remains that cherished candle in your being.

May God peace be with you through this terrible time. I am so very sorry you are experiencing this sorrow. All of you and Jin Joo deserve only joy in your lives I pray for all of you. God's comfort.

Lovingly, Virginia Wyland

A letter of condolences from one of her Seattle piano teachers.

Thanksgiving with a stranger

Izabela and Jin Joo went for groceries and returned with a young African-American man they invited to come home for Thanksgiving Dinner.

I was certainly surprised when he showed up.

Jin Joo wanted to share Thanksgiving with someone who had not been invited anywhere and was very excited to have brought him home.

They met him at the coffee shop at the University Village. He was well dressed and groomed. He told them he was a student and interested in writing a book.

As Izabela was always eager to share our teaching with others, she invited him later to our church in Ballard.

He came once or twice with his girlfriend. Unfortunately, communication with him was lost.

Jin Joo goes back to Korea in her Junior Year

In her junior year of High School (2000), Jin Joo traveled to Korea with twenty others from the Sun Hak Choir, founded by one of our members in Seattle. They had prepared many Korean songs for the 80th Birthday Celebration of Father Moon.

After the successful event, she called us and sent a letter explaining she wanted to stay in Korea for five months. She persuaded her best friend in Seattle to stay with her. They already had a place to stay and arranged to study for their high school program in Korea. They felt very comfortable there, so we agreed.

For room and board, they gave English lessons to the children of the family they stayed with. Having always regretted returning home when she got sick four years earlier, this was a way to redeem that experience. She was determined to accomplish a task when she decided on something.

Research on arranged marriages

From her early years, Jin Joo wanted an arranged marriage and to be matched with a spouse, as we were. She wanted to participate in the matching by Father Moon when she was sixteen, but we persuaded her to wait a few more years.

Just before her eighteenth birthday, Father Moon announced that from now on, the parents would be responsible for finding a spouse from among their unificationist community.

In February of 2002, she was matched to a son of our friends, born in the same year. They met for a second time in Korea and attended the Blessing of Marriage. After a short vacation, she returned to finish High School and he went to his country in South America, promising to see each other soon.

Because of that experience, her English teacher asked her to write a paper on 'Arranged Marriages.'

Jin Joo started interviewing couples from different religions about their arranged marriage journey. They were couples from the Hindu and Sikh faiths. She had seen firsthand how we, her parents, had fared through our arranged marriage. Like all marriages, we also have had difficulties as we learned to understand and accept each other. She witnessed a commitment that we promised not to break under any circumstances.

Eugene, you probably know that arranged marriages are prevalent throughout the world, especially in Islamic, Jewish, Hindu and Sikh traditions.

In those cultures, sexual purity before marriage is an essential requirement. Those who marry in this way have the attitude that they are not just marrying their spouse but also their spouse's family.

This is an extraordinary concept for the Western world, but it is a fact. The extended family is a big part of the marriage and becomes a support center. I knew this from an early age.

The essential attitude for couples in an arranged marriage is accepting their spouse as their life partner. These marriages emphasize the next generation, so the matching is a blending of characters to create children more balanced in character and spirit.

We are all told to be careful when you marry. Few can distinguish between good and bad characters when young and blind "in love." The bad boy is the one the girls chase because he is wild and exciting, but it doesn't take long to realize these boys don't stay around very long.

Young women especially need to be educated about purity because they ultimately decide to say "yes or no" in a relationship. Women are more vulnerable because they want to be loved and they mistakenly take the desire to have sex with love. Many are used and abused by men who eventually break their hearts. The statistics of those who live together before marriage or live without the covenant of marriage show it is detrimental to a lasting relationship. A man or woman who has experienced multiple relationships will find it difficult to forget those experiences and be challenged to love their present partner entirely.

Jin Joo understood this concept even at a young age and would talk to her friends about her one true love in the future.

As you know, Western culture has lost many Christian values. As cultures become more materialistic, people tend to worry more about earthly possessions and a comfortable lifestyle rather than spending quality time with their children. Very few women or men think about what kind of children will come from their sexual encounters or if their relationship will be "forever."

The free sex culture and readily available abortions destroy the ideal of God's centered life and family. Sadly, some lifestyles end within one generation and life and lineage cannot be continued.

I realize how fortunate our Unificationist younger generation is because they don't have to worry about finding a spouse. As parents are now involved in matching their young adults, the process differs significantly from when we were matched. Preparation classes, applications and medical exams are now required before somebody's name can be placed on a matching database. Young people are taught to improve themselves by overcoming any addictions before they can search for the right partner and first become a person "that you would like to spend your life with." I think it is excellent advice.

Nowadays, more time is available to communicate with a possible partner before making a final decision. What is essential is that parents from both families are included in the process. Parents can suggest a match, or young people can choose each other. It is now more similar to the matching process in other religious traditions.

The young people can concentrate on developing their character and talents and pursue academic interests until they are mature enough to be matched with a suitable partner that both families agree to.

Eugene, I have wondered if couples are happier in traditional Western marriages because they were once "deeply in love" or in arranged marriages that don't begin with "being in love."

Arranged marriages have fewer divorces than a "fall in love" and get married relationship. I believe it is because arranged marriages begin with an acceptance and desire to learn to love the spouse. There is no illusion that the other is perfect and that it will be a fairy tale story. If we want to succeed in our relationships, we must learn to make them work and learn how to unconditionally love the other, with a love that encompasses trust and forgiveness, given all of their and our faults.

Jin Joo interviewing the Sikhs' leader in the Renton Temple, Washington.

National Marine Fisheries Service

I was in Seattle when the pollock fishery was to open in January 1999. It had been several years since I had been back in Kodiak. I had just taken over the position of CEO and decided to go for the Pollock fishing opening to check how the company was doing.

I made reservations for Kodiak so that I would arrive the day before fishing would begin. Something came up unexpectedly and I had to change my flight plans to arrive in Kodiak the next day in the late afternoon, the opening day.

When I arrived in Kodiak, the Amber Dawn, a 110 foot trawler, one of the boats fishing for our plant, had already delivered fish twice that day. There was a new regulation by the National Marine Fisheries Service (NMFS), a federal agency responsible for the conservation and management of marine resources, that individual deliveries were not to exceed 300,000 pounds. Any overages were to be reported and the value of the excess was to be paid to the NMFS. It was a means to help them pay the costs of managing the fishery.

The Amber Dawn's first delivery in the morning was 312,464 pounds. Our production manager, who was not a church member and whom I had never met or talked to before because he reported only to the plant manager, decided to alter the fish ticket to reflect a delivery of just 296,115 pounds for the first delivery and add the additional poundage of 16,349 pounds onto the second delivery.

This infraction was discovered and reported to the NMFS by a disgruntled worker checking weights and working for the boats delivering to the plant. An investigation lasting two and a half years began and a felony case hung over my head as the government tried to implicate me in directing this fishery violation.

A fishery felony is a severe offense leading to a lengthy prison sentence. Given that it was only an infraction of $1,500 of fish in value and the first time the new regulation of 300,000 pounds maximum delivery was instituted, there would have been a slap on the wrist and a small fine if it were any other company. But we were the "Moonie" company and they planned to make us an example.

The NMFS investigator said that officials take civil action against fishermen and processing plants for violations, but criminal charges are rare. He said that authorities wanted to emphasize the importance of industry records in helping managers regulate fisheries and preserve fish stocks.

Our fish tickets reflected the correct amount of fish delivered that day, so his argument that they were concerned about records being correct was fallacious.

In the end, the fine for $1,500 of fish was blatantly extreme for a company whose books were in the red. Fines totaled $196,000 plus lawyer fees.

The NMFS offered me a sentence of eighteen months if I would admit my guilt, but I refused. I believe they wanted to showcase a Moonie along with the fine.

I said, "Take me to court and prove that I am guilty."

I knew that if the case was taken to trial and I was found guilty, I would receive a much longer sentence. Those two and a half years were very stressful for my wife and me as we worried I could end up in jail. We knew that going up against the government in court would be difficult following Father Moon's court case, – it was rigged from the start and he ended up in jail for a disputed $7,000.

During that time, I did my best to keep the company from going bankrupt.

If I had arrived in Kodiak the day before the fishery opened and been at the plant, even not knowing that the production manager had decided to falsify the fishery ticket, as the CEO of the company, I would have ended up in jail.

Looking back, was it fate that prevented me from taking the first flight reservation to Kodiak in 1999?

IRS case

The stress of the waiting and worry had been a significant event in Izabela's and my life.

Wondering if I would end up in prison didn't leave me for a long time. I couldn't forget how close I had come to the edge of a precipice. I wasn't concerned about my own life but more worried about how incarceration would impact my family. Without an income, it would have been a disaster.

I thought about Father Moon and his experience going to prison, being sentenced to eighteen months in Danbury prison in 1984. The photos showing him waving as he left for prison in Danbury, Connecticut, were heartbreaking and I wondered how he felt when he entered the prison. I believe, because he had been down that road before, he knew God was with him.

He was incarcerated a total of six times throughout his life. Once under the Japanese occupation regime and three times by the North Korean communists, once in the Republic of Korea and finally, the United States. He was in prison for a total of five years. His longest prison sentence was in the North Korean Hungnam Labour Prison. It was two years and eight months of hard labor, bagging a nitrogen sulfate fertilizer to be shipped to the Soviet Union. The substance was very caustic and caused blisters and wounds on the hands and body. Living on the meager rice and barley soup portions, most prisoners didn't survive longer than six months.

The injustice of his sentence stirred me to question how he could have been found guilty and jailed for only $7,000 of unpaid taxes on money to be used for church purposes, so technically, it was not taxable. Being his first tax return after arriving in America, it was truly unbelievable how the government had pulled that off. I spent a lot of time trying to understand how it all transpired.

Eugene, I was fortunate to find and read a book called *Inquisition* by Carlton Sherwood that explains why Father Moon wasn't given a fair trial and was framed by the government of the United States. Father Moon's defense requested a bench trial by a judge rather than a biased jury, but this was denied.

Inquisition is a detailed and unbiased account of Father Moon's tax evasion case. Carlton Sherwood was a professional investigative reporter who had worked for news organizations before working for *The Washington Times*. He felt there must have been something wrong and he began to work with a plan to uncover corruption within the Unification Church.

While working for *The Washington Times*, long after Father Moon had been convicted of income tax evasion and sentenced to eighteen months in federal prison, he launched his investigation. He searched internal church financial records, government files and court testimony for over two years. He interviewed dozens of people directly involved with church financial operations and realized nothing sinister was going on in the church. There were no lavish lifestyles, hidden bank accounts, no sexual scandals and no pervasive hypocrisy.

He concluded, "The Unification Church, its leaders and followers were and continue to be the victims of the worst kind of religious prejudice and racial bigotry this country has witnessed in over a century. Moreover, virtually every institution we as Americans hold sacred, the Congress, the courts, law enforcement agencies, the press and even the U.S. Constitution itself, was prostituted in a malicious, oftentimes brutal manner as part of a determined effort to wipe out this small but expanding religious movement."

Christian ministers from different denominations eventually came out in support of Father Moon because they realized it was possible that they could be next in line for the gavel. It was common practice in many churches for a pastor to hold church monies in his account for church purposes.

> *"The judge stated that he received perhaps one hundred letters from prominent church leaders, protestants and Catholics, decrying that a religious leader could be prosecuted for merely holding church funds in his name." Inquisition page 387*

As the judge mentioned, the jury of ten women and two men were uneducated and did not read, talk, or know much. To add to the disgrace, several had serious language difficulties twisting the dagger deeper, so they were not the jury anyone would want to decide your future if charged in a complicated tax case.

> *"The judge also stated that the jury could put aside their bias, which wasn't the case." Inquisition page 380*

The jury returned from a long deliberation over five days with a guilty verdict. Father Moon shook hands, thanked his lawyers and turned to shake the hand of the prosecutor, Martin Flumenbaum, but he gathered his papers and left. This was another example of forgiveness in Father Moon's heart for his enemy, as I'm sure he was forgiving America for its treatment of him. We had heard many stories in which he had forgiven those who had tortured him to the point of death.

The jury was clearly biased, as it was made known after the fact and Chapter 1 of the book *Inquisition* is about the secret tapes. These were tapes of a juror, Mrs. Steward, talking about the case to a friend over the phone and unbeknown to her, the conversation was being recorded.

She was sorry she voted for the defendant to be guilty when, in her heart and head, she felt there was insufficient proof of his guilt. She seemed to question if justice had been done to Reverend Moon. She also talks about the forelady, the one selected to speak for all the jurors, how she had been quite strong in convincing the jurors to vote guilty. The forelady tried to force and bully the others based on her biased opinions, saying things like, "he takes these kids' minds and twists them, brainwashes them. He doesn't want them to be with their families."

I believe the primary reason Father Moon was found guilty and sentenced was the insidious statement by the judge to disregard religion during the trial.

The whole defense strategy was trampled on in a New York minute after that statement.

After that one statement, how could his lawyers reasonably defend him and explain that all monies in his bank account were for religious purposes?

This was unbelievable, given that the man on trial was a religious leader who created a worldwide movement with thousands of followers.

The imprisonment of Father Moon was a major setback for the Unification Movement. Like being tarred and feathered, it is challenging to remove the tar later. In the future, an American President will hopefully posthumously pardon him for wrongful imprisonment.

I become incensed every time the media mention Father Moon's name because they always add in most articles or commentary that he was jailed for tax evasion while displaying the worst photo of him they can find, making him look like a charlatan. There is never any mention that he was imprisoned for a meager amount of about $7,000. Yes, it seems incredible to be jailed for eighteen months for $7,000 of unpaid taxes on money intended to be used for church purposes.

A Senate subcommittee chaired by Senator Orrin Hatch also conducted its own investigation into Reverend Moon's tax case and published its findings in a report that concluded:

> *"We accused a newcomer to our shores of criminal and intentional wrongdoing for conduct commonly engaged in by a large percentage of our religious leaders, namely, the holding of church funds in bank accounts in their names. Catholic priests do it. Baptist ministers did it and so did Sun Myung Moon.*
>
> *No matter how we view it, it remains a fact that we charged a non-English-speaking alien with criminal tax evasion on the first tax returns he filed in this country. We didn't give him a fair chance to understand our laws. We didn't seek a civil penalty as an initial means of redress. We didn't give him the benefit of the doubt. Rather, we took a novel theory of tax liability of less than $10,000 and turned it into a guilty verdict and eighteen months in federal prison.*
>
> *I do feel strongly that after my subcommittee has carefully and objectively reviewed this (Reverend Moon's tax) case from both sides, injustice rather than justice has been served. The Moon case sends a strong signal that if one's views are unpopular enough, this country will find a way not to tolerate but to convict. I don't believe that you or I or anyone else, no matter how innocent, could realistically prevail against the combined*

forces of our Justice Department and judicial branch in a case such as Reverend Moon's."

Eugene, while Father Moon was imprisoned, rather than harboring any resentment, he requested that booklets, letters and videotapes with Divine Principle teaching be mailed to 300,000 Christian leaders in America. *God's Warning to the World*, a book containing a compilation of seven of his speeches, was his message from prison. He was speaking as a prophet of God relaying a warning to America, given out of love, that it had not yet lived up to God's expectation.

He was concerned that a self-centered, materialistic America was liable to God's judgment. He urged American Christians to set an example of goodness, righteousness and sacrificial love for the rest of the world and to go beyond their denomination.

He mentions that the greatest puzzle in human history is how the name of Jesus, an unknown, without religious education, son of a carpenter, became known in every household in the last 2,000 years. He wasn't accepted in his lifetime. He didn't have a formal education and looked humble and shabby as he went from village to village. His followers were fishermen, tax collectors and harlots and people thought he was a blasphemer or crazy and dangerous. He was finally crucified on the cross, forgiving all those who had persecuted and rejected him.

Father Moon's message was a call to Christian ministers to awaken their spirits and realize who he was. Unfortunately, few could go beyond their literal interpretation of the Bible and their belief that Jesus' Second Coming would be a return on the clouds of heaven.

Prison Life – Danbury Spirit

Without any bitterness, Reverend Moon served time in Danbury Federal Prison. Initially, he was received coldly by the other inmates, most of whom had heard about him through newspaper articles or television reports.

Eugene, you understand the prison atmosphere. In only a few weeks, however, the other prisoners began to accept this Korean religious leader, not because he preached to them, which was forbidden by prison rules, but because he took the most unwanted jobs and worked with them cheerfully. His positive attitude toward life in prison began to command respect and even admiration from the other prisoners. Some of them began to come to him for counseling and advice.

Some of the inmates openly defended him. One of them, Ed Farmer, wrote a letter about his experiences with Father Moon in Danbury.

> *"I was fortunate. I only had to be in Danbury for three months. I knew I was going and I knew Reverend Moon was there. They had it in the paper every other day. I was curious. As it turned out, I was in the cubicle right next to his cell, five feet away. Moon has a very good sense of humor. It's hard for me to think of a person as being mean or brainwashing people with the sense of humor he has. He truly loves people. I mean, he likes being with them. He likes being kidded; he likes being teased. I never saw a mean act on his part. He never asked for special treatment. He mopped floors, cleaned tables and helped other people when he was finished with his job.*

When you'd be down in spirit, he'd come along, pat you on the back and smile and laugh. He doesn't put on a face today or put on generosity or kindness today and then not tomorrow. Reverend Moon is Reverend Moon, a very steady, ongoing force. I think that man could be happy wherever he went. He carries his religion with him. He doesn't need a book. Everyone feels it. It's very evident."

True World Foods

The company in Kodiak needed funding and the movement was already financially stretched and unable to supply capital. We found ourselves in a weak position, not unlike being in a war with an arm tied behind our back, trying to survive in every possible way. We tried everything to make the business profitable and in some years, we did have better success.

Because the company didn't qualify for financing through traditional banking routes because it wasn't solvent, we were forced to use a more expensive forms of financing to pay for payroll, fish deliveries, equipment, packaging cold storage fees, etc. – burdening the company's bottom line and speeding its death spiral.

Under the conditions in which we were working, it was only a matter of time before we would be forced to close our doors. I felt responsible for saving the company, which was analogous to a good sea captain who would find a safe harbor or go down with the ship. I had asked the president of our company to have a sister company take over the Kodiak business a number of times and he finally agreed.

I felt I had found a safe harbor when True World Foods Group, primarily managed by Japanese members, finally took control in 2001.

They had established a very successful fish distribution business, serving restaurants throughout America. I was relegated back to sales. They soon realized the fish processing business in Alaska was a tough nut to crack. We watched as many companies closed over the years and within three years, they decided to close the business before losing more money.

World Trade Center attack 9/11/2001

True World Foods took control of the Kodiak business in 2001 and their management team came to Kodiak to discuss the business. I came from Seattle.

We will all remember where we were when the World Trade Center towers were attacked on September 11th, 2001. Our meeting coincided with that disaster.

Father and Mother Moon were in Kodiak and we were all sitting in North Garden listening to Father speak.

He had been talking for a few hours when I noticed a buzz in the room. Someone had received a call on their cell phone. I knew something was happening as a few people were getting up and leaving.

No one wanted to interrupt, but as soon as Father finished speaking, he was informed of the tragedy and we turned on the TV.

What we saw looked like a movie. It was the most unbelievable sight unfolding before us, as we could see replay after replay of the planes crashing into the towers. I know everyone will never forget that terrible sight for the rest of their lives. We just couldn't believe that this was real. We all looked at Father.

He nodded and said, "Violence begets violence."

Eugene, Father Moon, looked so disappointed because he had worked tirelessly to work with leaders of different religions, especially Christians, Jews and Muslims. Missionaries were sent to over 120 countries in 1975, starting with Japan and the USA in the early 1960s. The first name of his movement was called Holy Spirit Association of World Christianity, not the Unification Church, which would indicate that it would be another Christian denomination. His life's work has been to build a world of peace by bringing the global family of humankind together. He said a few words in Korean, then got up and left. He was quiet for a few days. He didn't come out of his room. I was told he went into prayer.

He had predicted these problems and we, as a movement, desperately tried to unite the different religions through the international blessing movement and other interfaith initiatives.

There are three weaknesses of religious people:

- They are not realistic and are orientated towards the hereafter.
- They can be narrow-minded.
- They can be fanatical and this tragic attack was the most unbelievable example of being extreme and fanatical.

The world was looking at New York and the Pentagon in Washington, D.C., and witnessed the human spirit triumph in such a miserable situation as strangers helped each other. America came together, even for a short while and there was a feeling of comradeship.

During these times, we turn our hearts to God and again remember what is essential in our lives, families, friends and goodwill to others. We again got in touch with our souls.

My wife, together with others, attended a Mosque in the Northgate area of Seattle, supporting making it a "Hate Free Zone," offering flowers and protecting the building from possible attacks.

If we say we are religious people, we have to be the ones to overcome the lines of division that are crippling the human race. If we can live with a loving heart, all walls can be broken down. A true religion cares for all members of the human family. Only by forgiving our enemies and genuinely loving one another can we end the bloodshed and usher in an era of lasting peace.

"A World of Everlasting Peace is the desire of all people throughout the Ages." — Father Moon

Suicide bomber

God never wants us to strike back with vengeance and hate. It is sad to hear about suicide bombers strapping a bomb on themselves to kill innocent people because they believe they are martyrs who will be rewarded in "heaven." They will regret these murders at their own hands when they arrive in the next world.

How much more impact and change could they make if they could forgive and embrace their enemy?

The love bomb is the bomb that can change people's hearts, not the bomb of vengeance and violence, which will only produce more vengeance and violence. We hope that the next generation of children can learn this.

Eugene, there should be an exchange of marriage between enemies. Father Moon was guided to match and bless couples from enemy nations because he believed the exchange of marriage between enemies is the fastest and simplest way to tear down the differences and eventually bring world peace.

The Jews, Christians and Muslims have been taught to believe they should never intermarry.

But I have seen with my own eyes how hate and mistrust can change through international marriages.

"Peace Starts with Me" is where peace begins. Peace comes first through peace within the self, without any conflict between the spiritual mind and physical body. Through constant effort, we can create peace with others, our spouse and children, allowing peace in the family, society, nation and world.

Ultimately, there can be peace and understanding between religions.

Jin Joo's Essay, written for the UN Essay Contest in 2000

We decided to read this essay to everyone who attended one of the next memorials. It showed how important to her was a good marriage and family.

In the first few lines, she talks about how sorry she felt for those who took drugs and killed people. How she wrote about this was uncanny and it happened to her.

> *When I start thinking about the problems of this world, my heart aches for the starving children in Africa, the people in this world who feel no*

love, people who would rather take than give and kids who do drugs and kill people.

Why are there health problems, different global issues, political conflicts and countries not uniting? How wonderful it would be if we could find a solution to solve all these problems. Despite all the terrible things happening in this world, what we can improve is to learn to love and help others in need. Everybody wants to be loved and wants to love and help someone.

Where does true love originate? We can say that it is "implanted" in us from the heart of our Creator. That's what makes us humans. The first place we experience love is the family through the unconditional love of our parents and grandparents if we are lucky to know them.

Sadly, many marriages in Western culture end in divorce. How can happiness and love exist when we don't know how to create strong and committed families?

Today, many single moms, dads and children feel neglected and unwanted. So, after much thinking, I decided one thing that would make our world a better place would be to create strong, loving families.

How to achieve that is the question.

I believe in experiencing God's love in the family so much that I would start to teach people how precious a family truly is. I am a shy person in public, but I feel an urge to give people the key to being happy and loved.

I come from a family with both parents and three siblings. Honestly, I am grateful that my parents are together and I am sure that divorce is not an option.

It would be a struggle to live with my mom during the week, stay with my dad during the weekend and be separated from my siblings. It is a good feeling knowing your parents are happy together, loving and respecting each other. It is a great feeling to grow up in a loving atmosphere. When I look around today, few people experience true love and happiness.

Having a strong family and knowing you are loved can stop you from looking for love elsewhere. There are many different ways in which I see people looking for love or comfort and some fulfill this need by rebelling, taking drugs, or committing crimes. This is what is happening every single day and why? Because there is not enough true love in the family.

Family is so important to me. I want a great future family with kids who can see my husband and me loving and respecting each other. I want my kids to grow up feeling loved so that when they are older and move on, they can carry that ideal of true love and happiness and show that to their future spouses, children, friends and community.

How can this true family be created? It's not easy. When couples are in love and get married, they rarely think about the possibility of future disagreements or divorce. Unfortunately, many, even in Christian communities, fail to stay together despite the promises made to each other.

I think more groups need to promote family values in schools, churches, communities and other social organizations. By having these groups, we can prevent many issues in this world caused by the breakdown of families.

God's Love can be experienced in a True Family.

Will Jin Joo go to Heaven?

It was decided that Jin Joo's memorial service would be in Washington, D.C.

As we drove there from Charlotte, North Carolina, receiving many calls from family and friends with their condolences was a comfort.

One was a call from a dear friend. She asked, "Do you think Jin Joo will go to heaven?"

I was astonished that she would ask such a question, but she was a Christian and believed that if you aren't saved through faith in Jesus, you will not go to heaven. I said, "Don't worry, she will be there, without a doubt."

Eugene, I thought, would I see her in the spiritual world when it was my turn to go? Jin Joo was a much purer soul than me. Could I care about others like she did? The more pure spirits must deserve to occupy the higher realms in that world.

The Unification teaching is similar to the Catholic doctrine concerning whether or not a spirit will go to heaven. It is based on whether they were free from sin and had lived a good life, whereas the Christian belief is that you have to be saved in order to go to heaven, a much easier and more convenient "get in free" card.

What is the spiritual world like?

Sensitive people who have had glimpses into the world beyond say it is a world much like our own but having no time nor space as we think of these dimensions; it exists in a higher dimension of energy and, in its higher realms, is a world of inexpressible beauty. It is a world of endless possibilities for creativity and full realization of self; it is a world where the love of God is like the air we breathe. As air is the atmosphere on earth, God's love is the atmosphere in the spirit world.

One's spirit self can travel with thought waves. Therefore, if one thinks of a person and place, he can immediately be transported there. Communication is also by thought. In addition, one is free from the restrictions of the physical body. In the spiritual world, one realizes that life on earth has been preparation for a fuller, freer, richer, eternal existence.

From *"Near Death Experience Research"* by Nora Spurgin

Message from the spiritual world

David, a member with the same last name, drove immediately to Charlotte upon hearing about Jin Joo. His family was still grieving due to the death of seventeen-year-old Andrew, who had been killed in a car accident the year before. David wanted to be there for us because he knew what we were going through.

Eugene, It was uncanny how Andrew Byrne died the year before in the same month. His father, Sean, was the first Catholic priest to join our movement many years before.

We were later given a message from the spiritual world through a medium from Andrew that life on earth is very brief. People are created to live on earth for a fleeting moment and then go to the next world. Your standard of values and your life activities during your time on earth determine your position in the spiritual world.

How terrible is it to think one goes into the next world when they have abused and misused people in this world and all is visible in the next world? In this world, we have the illusion of a world of substance, space and time surrounding us. We go about our daily activities sure that we are in a contained environment. Like a child in the womb who does not know that it has to move out when all his organs are ready to face birth into the world of air.

But the world is not contained. It is just space and everything is in constant motion, constant change. This is the illusion, like when we are in a crib and think this is the whole world. We feel secure and safe in this environment. When we are out of it, we are usually in the warm embrace of our parents and we are sure this is the whole world.

But as we grow up and move out of the crib, we realize our limited consciousness. Still, it served us at that age. But it cannot serve us now in the broader environment. Most people live today as if there is no afterlife and this earthly life is all there is. They don't understand that throughout our life on this earth, our good or bad deeds influence the growth of our spirit and that decides where we end up after death.

Memorial Ceremony

We all came together to celebrate Jin Joo's wonderful life. Her friends came from all over, some coming from other countries.

One of her friends smelled a strong scent of roses as he drove to the memorial. Did Jin Joo like roses? He asked. Someone else mentioned that she always sprayed herself and others with rose water before they went out for the day.

In our way of life and tradition, death shouldn't be a sorrowful occasion. It is easier said than done. The death process should be understood as a rebirth into another world, like a butterfly ridding itself of the shackles of its cocoon and becoming a new body, existence and entity. It is not merely ascension and change but Heavenly harmony, like the evaporation of water – it is still water but in a different form.

We stood close to her coffin and I could feel pride in my heart for her. Even though there were so many temptations as she grew up, she always did the right thing. She struggled with decisions that weren't easy but always decided what was right, even when she knew it would challenge her.

I felt deep sorrow as I thought about how she wouldn't be able to have a husband and raise a happy family.

There was a beautiful picture of her in the front and I just kept my attention on her eyes. They looked out at me with compassion and heart and I felt how much she loved me.

I felt some regret as I thought about our lives together. I should have hugged her more. I was grateful I never had to spank her as she was growing up.

I would have done anything to reclaim those moments together again.

Dr. George and his wife attended the Ceremony.

I had not seen him for many years since we had worked together in New York. He had joined the movement earlier than me and was one of the first friends I met while working on the construction crew when I joined. He welcomed me by giving me a circular saw to add to my tools. He had a doctorate in computerology and was capable of doing anything in the construction trades.

During the ceremony, he approached me in tears. I had heard that he was having health problems.

When we shook hands, I could feel something in his hand.

I said, "Doctor George, I know what that is."

The week before I had been thinking of buying a small Swiss army-type knife and I knew what lay between our hands was the same. This was one of those rare and beautiful connections of heart between friends and I again felt the love and presence of God comforting me.

Fort Lincoln Cemetery

Jin Joo was laid to rest in Fort Lincoln cemetery in Washington D.C., America's capital city. Our movement has established an area where our members can be buried.

The person responsible for developing this area kindly showed me a plan of available plots and asked us where we would like Jin Joo to be placed. We chose the front row in the middle as a more accessible location for those who would come to pay their respects.

Father and Mother Moon recognized her life of faith and dedication by giving her an eternal name, Sun Mi Nyo, which means "Daughter of Goodness and Beauty" in Korean.

We were very moved and honored when we received this beautiful calligraphy, seldom given to anyone. We knew that Jin Joo would be proud.

"Daughter of Goodness and Beauty" was fitting for Jin Joo because she had a pure heart and was dedicated to sexual purity even amid all that went on at her school, what was portrayed in Hollywood movies and society in general.

Father Moon wrote this calligraphy in Kodiak, Alaska. We later realized a photo taken as a family with Father and Mother Moon in Kodiak in 1989 was taken on the exact month and day this calligraphy was written. It was hand-carried from Kodiak and presented to us for Jin Joo.

Jin Joo's closest friends spent the day before her funeral writing a song to honor her. Standing under the tent next to Jin Joo's casket, they sang "Pearly Whites."

Listening to music conceived through love for our daughter was profoundly moving. I could feel the heart of God as he had hope for goodness and beauty to spread to the world.

Eugene, as I stood looking at our daughter's casket, my heart went out to all the mothers and fathers who have had to endure such a painful and debilitating experience. I thought of all the many young men and women throughout history who died far too young in wars, sickness and accidents, to name just a few of the tragedies of life. I realized I was not alone, but a history of tears had swept through time.

Now was the time of mourning. How would we recover from such a terrible reality? How would we go on as a couple and family? Our hearts were breaking as we remembered our precious times with Jin Joo.

Sun Mi Nyo Mansei
Daughter of Goodness and Beauty, Mansei!

We didn't have the chance to say goodbye and say we love you and always will. We regretted not spending enough time together and had the false thought that we could do that in the future, which is sadly illusionary for many of us. There would have been beautiful joys that we would now be unable to experience. We would never be grandparents to her children or see the beauty of her family. We had such hope for her happiness and she had such an extraordinary passion for a loving husband and family.

The burial ceremony at the cemetery was profoundly moving. Joshua, a staff member of STF had brought his guitar. We sang to celebrate her life of goodness, prayed and said goodbye.

Everybody paid their respects, each laying a flower upon her casket. When I saw the many young people filing past her coffin, I felt hope for God because I could sense their purity and dedication. I saw the wisdom of God before my eyes. Here were the children from parents who had participated in the same mass wedding as our own, who were pure and dedicated.

I prayed about what I could say to our brothers and sisters to console them. It was a terrible shock for our community because they had never experienced a member of the younger generation being murdered. Few young women in history were so pure as her. She had given up her self-centered desires to join a year or two-year missionary program to practice the life of living for others.

She went to the spiritual world at the highest and purest point. It was a devastating shock to our Movement. We all felt vulnerable and I'm sure other parents were thinking, How would they handle the loss of their child in this way?

I spoke about the vivid dream I had the night before. In the dream, I had the experience of dying as a sinful man. It was a terrifying feeling as I felt regret and fear as my spirit left my body. That dream changed me forever.

This was a very special occasion in August of 1989 to take a family photo with Father and Mother Moon.

I'm sure it wasn't easy to listen to my talk, but I felt I should share this with those present. We cannot take fame, fortune, or knowledge to the next world. All we bring is our spirit and the heart and love we developed during a lifetime. How happy and unafraid you would be on the path of death knowing that you had served and helped people and had given everything to make a better world.

Jin Joo knew her spirit could develop through loving God and loving others through her good deeds. Her kindness, generosity and care helped her to achieve a bright spirit that could now travel freely to protect and care for those she loved.

We all hope to leave this physical world with such a beautiful spirit. Still, we were devastated and felt terribly lonely as we drove away, leaving her body at the cemetery.

A storm raged

On the night of Jin Joo's disappearance, Hyung Jin the youngest son of Father and Mother Moon was worried about his mother's life. This was the last day of her speaking tour in Japan.

The day was dark and a storm had kicked in. He had a bad feeling as the storm raged. Most days, he would spend hours in prayer outside, but on this day, he stayed inside. His prayer table outside was crushed as a tree broke loose during this storm and he felt there was turbulence in the heavens.

Memorial Service at Summit, Jin Joo's High School

Our family was invited to a Memorial celebrating her life. The Principal, teachers and students attended it.

Memorial for Jin Joo at Summit High School, Seattle.

A tree was planted and a bench with her name was installed overlooking the playgrounds.

We felt so much love from her teachers and friends and we presented them with the Indian Ten Commandments, which they mounted at school.

Pure Love Alliance

In the summer of 2000, Jin Joo Ellen decided to go on another Pure Love Alliance tour, this time traveling through the USA, France, Germany and England.

To pay for the trip, she and her friend worked as fish processors for the Bristol Bay salmon season in Egegik, Alaska.

She loved the experience of working with the fish and even loved the smell of the fish because she said it reminded her of the smell of my clothes coming home from working long hours in the fish processing plant.

The Pure Love Alliance was a youth ministry program developed to promote living for the sake of others while free of drugs and alcohol. It portrayed a new culture of sexual abstinence and purity before marriage and fidelity in marriage.

The sexual act, as Father Moon taught, is the most precious gift from God because it brings a man and woman together in the most personal and intimate way.

The group of probably over one hundred young high school-age boys and girls traveled, having rallies and speaking out about love and sex being too precious to be given away freely. They shared how they would wait and prepare for this special person and share a love and sexual experience only through the sanctity of marriage.

Unfortunately, in many cultures, sex has been turned into that which is dirty and degrading.

Eugene, as you probably know, pornography is such an epidemic, destroying the innocence of our youth exposed at every turn, making it difficult to have a pure relationship with one partner. The environment and culture of drugs, violence and sex try their best to wipe away all that is pure and good and choke the pure heart and soul within.

They made it to France and here is the photo with the famous Eiffel Tower.

Testimony from Robin, her Kodiak friend

This is Robin. I'm sorry I haven't tried to reach you sooner. I thought about it, but I just didn't know what I would say. I received your email about Jin Joo and I can't wait to see the book you speak of.

I miss your family a lot because we saw each other so many times when we were both in Kodiak. Jin Joo and I both had strong characters and, when we were with a group of our friends, we usually ended up dividing the group between my side and hers. But when we were alone, we often had a great time. It was interesting.

Then she moved away and the next time I saw her was that summer she came to work in Egegik. We had grown up a lot and just clicked from day one of that period. We had such a great time together and I started to see what a beautiful person she was, as did everyone else at the camp.

Everyone liked her because she was innocently sweet, genuinely sincere, thoughtful, excitable, fun and helpful. She got along with everyone she met and was an absolute pleasure to work with.

I remember her telling me how excited she was to go "processing" (fish) and I was like, "Are you kidding me?" I don't remember her complaining during that time, although I remember complaining a lot. I remember her laughing and having fun doing the dishes together in the big kitchen while listening to her soundtrack.

Initially, I thought, "This girl is so naive," because she talked about pure love to all those horny male processors we worked with. But I think she had won the respect of all those she worked with closely by the time we left, including myself.

When I heard she was coming to STF, now called GPA (Global Peace Alliance), I was so happy because I was looking forward to hanging out with her again.

Anyways, that's the Jin Joo I remember.

I hope you are doing okay, Mrs. Byrne. Again, I'm sorry I haven't tried to reach you earlier, but I didn't know what to say. Anyway, I hope to hear from you.

Sincerely,

Robin

Having a moment of rest from cleaning and racking salmon for freezing.

The essay "Evaluation of my character"

This essay was written for her senior class assignment.

I put myself in situations where I can grow and experience things. Last summer, I worked at a fish processing plant. I worked long and hard hours. I've never worked so hard in my entire life, but I thoroughly enjoyed it.

My dad worked for a fish business. At one point in his career, he processed fish, too, so I wanted to experience a taste of what he went through. Being an optimistic person, I made the best out of my situations. It was a great three weeks and I always find myself reminiscing about my experiences there.

One person who helped me grow tremendously is my dad. Whenever I do something incorrect, he doesn't blame me or excuse me, but he kindly explains what I did wrong, making me want to do better. He is extremely understanding and I feel I would be lost without him.

People need someone who smiles and gives them the freedom to be themselves and be independent. I'm incredibly grateful to my dad for giving me many opportunities to grow and travel the world. He has made a significant impact on who I am today.

Media interview

Eugene, the media called Judy Williams, a founder of Mothers of Murdered Offspring (MoMO) who knew your mother, to arrange the interview with us.

For more than twenty-five years, she made a profound impact on the families of murder victims and helped create violence prevention programs in Charlotte, North Carolina.

Jin Joo speaking at the famous Speakers' Corner in Hyde Park, London, England.

We agreed to meet them at our friend's house where we were staying. The Unification Movement has not received fair coverage by the media throughout the years. I was worried that, as members, we would be on the receiving end of biased and nasty press during the interview.

Eugene, We were definitely on the defensive when we met with them. Still, my wife saved the day by asking the interviewers to first watch the video of Jin Joo speaking in Hyde Park at the famous Speakers' Corner so they could get a sense of who she was as a young woman. She was sixteen then and throughout her teenage years, she was committed to purity.

The video showed her spirit as she called out to the crowd to stay abstinent from drugs and free sex and to be pure and prepare for this one special person to create a loving family.

The interviewer had tears in his eyes and was very kind when he asked us questions about her.

The Decision to Forgive

Eugene, I felt very strongly that we needed to forgive you as soon as possible for your sake and ours. I had always thought that if someone harmed my family, I would kill them myself.

But now there was a feeling that it was important to forgive you. I felt the heart of Jesus as he forgave those who killed him. I felt the heart of God as he looked upon the death of his son as he wanted to strike out at the human race, but because of the heart of Jesus, he forgave.

I felt that Jin Joo's heart was forgiving you and that she had no malice towards you, so I could also forgive you. I was told it would be better to wait to visit you, but I felt we needed to forgive you personally, so we came by train to Charlotte.

The night train ride to Charlotte

We took the train to Charlotte that evening.

I wanted to prepare myself for the possible meeting the next day with you. I bought the book *The Underground Railroad* to understand more about the history of African-Americans in the United States.

We know how painful it is to be a victim of prejudice. We decided we didn't look for vengeance but were determined to be an example to others.

We went to the jail to meet you and found it impossible as the visiting days were only once a week. The scheduled day had been the day before.

Meeting your mother, grandmother and aunt

Eugene, I felt it was essential to try to visit your family because we knew how bad your family must have felt to know that their son had killed someone.

We asked if there was any way to find out if you had family in the area. We received a call from Judy Williams of MoMO informing us that your mother lived close to where you met Jin Joo and would meet with us.

We wanted to protect your family from the media, so we quietly arranged a meeting with your mother and grandmother at their house.

I knew that the most painful burden was on your mother. I can't imagine the feeling of a mother, father and family knowing that their loved one has killed another. We all have such great hopes and expectations for our children.

We were almost involved in two accidents as we drove to meet Judy, who would take us to your mother's house. I felt that there was a presence that didn't want this meeting to happen and we would have crashed if I had the slightest feeling I didn't want to meet your mother, grandmother and aunt.

When my wife embraced your mother, I could see the tremendous pain and shame on your mother's face.

It was difficult for her even to look up and face us. We could see that she was religious and could only imagine that raising three sons alone was challenging.

We were surprised to see she was wearing a T-shirt with a big white cross similar to the T-shirt Jin Joo had worn in a skit two days before her death. Her performance symbolized fighting against evil and the unification of religion centered on Christianity.

It was difficult for Izabela to come to that meeting. I told her she didn't have to come, it was her decision. I was very proud of her as she hugged your mother with compassion. She could feel your mother's pain.

I wondered how many mothers could hug the mother of the son who had murdered their child. I could feel the real presence of God as we watched with awe this incredible sight as a black mother and a white mother, both in the worst pain imaginable, hugged each other. I knew then that God had given me an extraordinary wife.

We all walked across the road from their house to a small park. I walked with your grandmother holding her hand and Izabela with your mother. Judy Williams brought many purple balloons, which we released. They floated in the blue like doves, healing our broken hearts.

Finally meeting you

Eugene, I was surprised – my heart went to you as you entered wearing the prison orange suit. Here I saw a person in the worst possible pain of remorse and visibly, there was a fight within you. Our communication was short because you were only allowed to visit with us briefly.

You expressed how sorry you were and shared that Jin Joo was such a kind person. In the short walk you took together, she tried to help you change your life. You felt it was important to tell us that she was a virgin before she died.

As you mentioned, you should not have been released from jail when you were arrested eleven times before for other minor crimes. As you turned around and we waved goodbye, I could see a heavy burden lift from your heart as you returned the wave with a smile.

I walked away from the prison feeling overwhelmed and hopeless as we felt the immense tragedy of the human spirit expressed in one life.

My heart went out to all the people in prisons who had made such bad choices in their lives. I know that the jails are filled with people who feel sorry for what they have done to others, their families and themselves. I am sure that most feel this way if they are normal. Many have given up hope for themselves and believe they are evil. We believe that each person among us desires to seek out goodness. A desire that is settled deep within our original mind.

So, even in death, Jin Joo taught us a lot. She always saw the goodness in others. My whole life has been a search for God. I have come to many roadblocks and detours in that search. I am surprised that through the act of forgiving you for killing our daughter, I have come to realize the God within me finally. We are all to be the living temples of the living God.

I often think about Jin Joo. Strangely, my mind and heart still don't allow me to believe that she has died. My heart breaks whenever I think of how she died in that filthy little abandoned apartment. I can't embrace or see her with her children, with the husband she fervently dreamed about.

Even though life is callous for some of us, we must continue to love others. I now understand a parent's pain when losing their child.

Many blame God for their misfortunes and finally give up on their faith, but this isn't the world he envisioned. He waits for people to embody his heart and love to free and heal this world. God can work miracles if he can find just a few good people.

God doesn't need numbers. Looking back through history, we can see how a handful of exceptional people changed the course of history.

Visited by evil spirits

A few days after arriving back from Charlotte, Izabela and I were lying in bed, feeling immense sadness, trying to come to terms with the loss of Jin Joo. Suddenly, a cold chill came over me.

We both could sense an evil presence in the room. Our senses were overwhelmed by a terrible smell of what I imagine was like rotting flesh. I felt that a very evil spirit, if not Satan himself, had visited us.

I cried out in the dark for Satan to get out. He had no place in our holy home.

We quickly moved upstairs and slept in Jin Joo's room for the night.

Was it because we had the heart of forgiveness that an evil presence came to us?

An evil spiritual world has immense power

When we study history, there are many examples where evil spirits have used man to do unspeakable acts of cruelty to their fellow humans.

There is an evil force working in the world. It sounds too fairy tale, but we all experience fighting with a force that tries to push us against our very conscience.

Before I came to America, I was very interested in how the American people lived. Young New Zealanders had a negative attitude toward Americans at that time.

It's pretty apparent if it hadn't been for the Americans in the Second World War, history would have seen bloodshed like no one could imagine. Tyranny would have marched unstopped to eradicate any resemblance of goodness in the world. America helped to stop that march of madness and terror.

Hitler's ultimate purpose was to expand German territory, eliminate all European Jews and Gypsies and create a superior race of white people with blue eyes. I have wondered how most of the German people at the time could have collaborated in that madness to eliminate other races of people.

Would I have stood up in opposition or bowed down in fear for my own life, as many had done? If we raise our young people without morals, principles, heart and conscience, we will produce a generation without a heart and compassion for others.

God cannot forget America because of its young men and women's sacrifice. The world would have fallen into darkness if evil hadn't been stopped.

In WWI and WWII, the Korean War, the Vietnam War and other conflicts, America sacrificed its best young men and women for the freedom of others. It is still the most significant contributor to aid throughout the world. The real heart and greatness of America are the people. There is a hidden attitude to do what is right when required and a strong national pride, especially within the older generation.

Eugene, America, is unique because it is a melting pot of all people worldwide. It can be an example of unity and peace to the rest of the world. Where else can you find so many nationalities, races, cultures and religions living together in one country? It's a real "melting pot" where we can learn to accept others.

We are still facing problems, but the situation can improve because of our freedom. We are naturally stretched culturally to accept those who are different. No other country in the world has welcomed so many immigrants clamoring to come into this country because of the opportunity for anyone to prosper here if they put their mind to it.

The difficulty is that it takes the immigrants many years to realize finally that this is their country. I love and am proud of America and consider it my country now. It wasn't an overnight change in my thinking but a gradual transformation over the years.

District Attorney

Eugene, we decided to fight for your life and told the district attorney we opposed the death penalty because you needed time to improve spiritually and educate your conscience before you died.

Marsha Goodnow, the district attorney, had a daughter about the same age as Jin Joo. I could feel her anger and determination to get justice for Jin Joo's death.

We met with her and the detectives handling the case. She mentioned that they would seek the death penalty because abduction, theft, sexual assault and murder were all the ingredients that would justify that penalty.

They explained that a great struggle took place and that it looked like Jin Joo had fought and lost her life to protect her virginity. Her body was found naked. She was so passionate about true love and was saving herself for her one true love. It would have destroyed her if she had been raped and lived. Many unfortunate women today emotionally struggle because they were raped or abused as a child.

We explained at the meeting that we were against the death penalty in this particular situation and asked if they would take our plea for jail time only. We believe the family of the deceased should be considered before a sentence of death is decided. If a victim's family wishes to find closure through execution, that should be their decision.

We have chosen the opposite, love and forgiveness, releasing our souls from hate and vengeance that would have consumed us for the rest of our lives.

Conscience

Eugene, the only way I can understand and, in a way, accept this terrible loss, is that I strongly believe in a dark force that is more vicious and dangerous than we could ever possibly understand. This is why we can destroy ourselves and others and feel no regret or pain.

We can't imagine how bad we could be if we didn't have a God-centered conscience of caring, loving and respecting each other.

When our spiritual mind is in perfect harmony with that conscience, then God dwells in us. For many, the physical body's desires are stronger than their conscience and the body leads them to an unending pursuit of external, physical pleasures, which can never satisfy the inner hunger of man's soul.

Drugs, alcohol, all other vices and lack of religious or moral upbringing blanket our conscience and the evil, ego-centered selfish nature in each of us shows its ugly head and we cave into that evil nature. The body acts like a raging bull, leaving devastation in its wake.

Waiting for sentencing

Eugene, I had a great fear that you would be sentenced to death.

This was a heavy burden that we felt for nearly a year. I had decided to be at the execution if there was to be one, not out of vengeance but to be with you in prayer.

We felt distraught about your life. We couldn't imagine going through the torment of waiting for your execution. I can only imagine the terrible pain and fear as a family waits for the day of the execution of their loved one.

We received a call on my birthday, July 1st, from the District Attorney explaining the sentence of forty years without parole.

One mistake

Eugene, it's frightening to think about how quickly someone can mess up their life. All it takes is one mistake to destroy our plans, goals and future happiness.

I was fortunate that my mother emphasized that advice when I was young. I am glad I listened to her. It has served me well in my life.

As temptations have come up, I always remember what dear old mom would say: "It only takes one instance to mess up your life. It applies to all aspects of life. Most important is the decision on the one you marry and to be faithful in that marriage."

I was flying to Seattle from the East Coast, with a changeover in Denver. When you are at your weakest, temptation always seems to visit.

I was sitting next to a woman about fifteen years younger than me. She had her headset on, listening to music and didn't even acknowledge me as I sat beside her.

After an hour into the flight, she took the headset off and I noticed she was listening to one of my favorite musicians, Jesse Cook, a flamenco guitarist.

I told her I studied classical guitar for a year when I was younger and loved the romantic Spanish guitar music.

She became very friendly and we talked for the rest of the flight. We had a lot in common and it was the most pleasant conversation I had in a long time.

When we arrived in Denver, we walked together into the terminal and she said she was staying there overnight and asked me if I would like to have dinner with her.

I felt young again and I am ashamed to say it took me too long to tell her I should stick to my original flight. I thought it was best not to ask for her phone number and we said goodbye. I could have destroyed my marriage and my family if I had followed my feelings.

Leaving the Fish Business after Twenty Years

After Jin Joo passed, I couldn't concentrate or have the heart to make sales. My wife was sick and I thought it best to make a complete change, but I didn't want to leave the company without sales in Seattle.

I called Kenji, with whom I had worked well for twenty years in the fish business. I told him I was thinking of leaving the company for my family's sake. I asked him if he could come to Seattle and include U.S. and European sales in his duties. I also felt sorry for him and his family, who had lived in Kodiak for so long. I thought it would be good for them to make a change. I would explain my customer base and all business matters before I left.

Because the Chinese market had opened up to purchase headed and gutted fish, our company was now undergoing changes. We were able to minimize the processing of filets, which saved on labor costs.

Kenji came to Seattle and took over from me. Unfortunately, he died of lung cancer about a year later. He never smoked or drank his whole life.

Going back to New Zealand

We needed to heal as a family, so in the fall of 2004, we moved to New Zealand, another major change in our lives.

Initially, we stayed with my brother, who lived a few houses away from my parents. I was happy my children could get to know their grandparents and extended family. They had a glimpse of what I experienced while growing up. We were staying on a peninsula and I felt at home as I could see the ocean's magnificence surrounding us.

We had left a Seattle summer to be greeted by another where we could swim in the warmer waters of New Zealand, which we couldn't do in the frigid waters of Puget Sound. It was like being on a summer holiday, but we couldn't fully enjoy it without Jin Joo.

The sound of the waves breaking and the constantly moving waves captured my gaze and the aroma in the air intrigued my senses. I never felt alone as the ocean cleaned my spirit.

Father Moon donated twenty-eight foot boats to Unification Centers in 120 countries. The larger countries received four boats and the smaller ones received two.

They were built by a sister company in New York. He helped design the prototype, a deep V hull that could handle rough waters. He spoke often about how the ocean would feed the hungry in the future. In the 1980s, he established a new organization, Ocean Church, to train young people in marine activities.

Izabela was able to go tuna fishing in Gloucester, Massachusetts, in 1978 when she joined the fish business in Norfolk, Virginia. It was her opportunity to be on the ocean as she had always dreamed about.

She and another woman went fishing with an experienced captain every day for a month and they caught three giant bluefin tuna, approximately 1,000 pounds each, during that time. That was an unforgettable experience that she often reminisces about.

It was sad to discover that the New Zealand Movement couldn't manage the two boats they had received. They had asked the local Sea Scouts, a personal development program association dedicated to boating and water-based activities for young people, to use the church boats to train their members. An agreement was made for an equal responsibility to pay for the upkeep and maintenance.

The two boats were moored in an estuary and I visited the Sea Scouts facility to survey the boats. They told me the boats weren't being used because of mechanical problems. I was surprised to find both boats in deplorable condition, weather-beaten and damaged.

Driving home, I imagined how disappointed Father Moon would be to see the boats in that condition. What if he visited and asked to go fishing? I decided I would fix both boats. After a few weeks, we returned and towed the first boat to the Gulf Harbor Marina in Whangaparaoa peninsula, north of Auckland, which was very close to my parents' house.

We decided the church would pay the marina fees and I would volunteer the labor. When the boat was lifted out of the water, we found extensive growth, which would have eventually destroyed the hull. There was much to do to repair the external and mechanical issues.

Working out in the sun by the water surrounded by beautiful boats somehow healed my heart. Our son helped a few times.

After repairing the second boat, I decided to try fishing at night because the long-line Russian fishermen from Alaska fished the nights with great success. One of my younger brothers came with me. We were out fishing until about 11:00 p.m. without success and decided to head back to the marina.

When I turned the key to fire the engine, nothing happened, not even a click. I thought it couldn't be a battery problem because we had two batteries, one for the deck lights and the other for the starter. It was very worrying as the weather was getting rough.

I opened up the engine compartment, searching for loose wires or anything out of the ordinary. My experience troubleshooting electrics was to go back to basics, starting at step one. The control looked out of gear, but it had been slightly moved to place it into gear, not allowing the engine to turn over. In neutral, she roared into life and we pulled up anchor and headed back.

The perspex screen on the windshield was damaged. Someone had previously tried to clean it with something abrasive, which made it dull and hard to see through – particularly at night, we were traveling almost blind. My brother sat in the front with his legs over the bow, directing me home. He would wave right or left as we headed for the entrance to the marina.

I suddenly felt something wasn't right and turned the boat firmly to starboard and was horrified as I looked back to see the marina breakwater made from huge rocks stacked on top of each other, looming above the water not more than twenty feet away.

If I hadn't followed my intuition and turned, we would have crashed into the rocks at twenty-five knots with my brother's legs hanging over the side. My mistake was that I had relied on my brother to direct me.

He was shocked and asked how I'd known to turn the boat.

I told him, "God did."

Damn, that was close. It wouldn't have been pretty if we had collided with hard rock. I realized my mistake was looking at the lights in the marina and not the ones at the entrance and I shouldn't have gone at night with a windshield I couldn't see through. Unfortunately, both boats were later sold.

The decision to return to the USA

We stayed in New Zealand for over a year.

In February of 2005, at the beginning of the school year, we rented a very nice modern house close to schools, shopping centers and close to our Movement's offices. Our three teenagers started to attend school.

It was a considerable shift moving to a different country, going to single-sex schools with uniforms and a new school system to navigate. The school program was based on twice-a-year exams and no homework. It was very different from the system in the U.S., where students were evaluated by submitting homework and doing well on tests.

Interestingly, the senior class in an all-girls school was required to wear long skirts throughout the school year. The girls were able to make new friendships pretty quickly.

For our fourteen-year-old son, it was not easy to make new friends and he missed his friends in Seattle. Our oldest daughter graduated from High School in New Zealand.

Eugene, New Zealand, is one of the most expensive countries in the world. House prices were the highest in the world due to immigrants coming to settle there. I realized that I couldn't live on a wage and didn't have the heart to start a plumbing business there, so we decided to return to America.

It wasn't only a financial decision but also a cultural one. I had to protect my teenagers.

New Zealand had become very liberal since I had left thirty years before. The drinking age was lowered to eighteen, so there were real problems with alcohol for youth and those issues follow many into their older age. Legalized prostitution and the new culture had changed the country.

Our girls had to walk past brothels to and from school. Drugs were destroying the youth as they did in America. There were no religious underpinnings in the culture anymore and anything was up for grabs. Divorce was common and marriage was outdated. We were constantly introduced to a partner rather than a wife or husband.

I realized that New Zealand had changed too much. It didn't feel like my country anymore and I realized I had become a proud American.

Jin Joo was buried in America and I thought we should live in the same land. I also wanted to work again with the fish business, so we left New Zealand looking for how God would guide our lives in America again.

Returning to Seattle in 2006

It wasn't easy for me to leave my New Zealand family again. I had always missed the summers and the joy of swimming at the beaches in the warm waters surrounding the New Zealand shoreline.

My children had missed their friends in America and wanted to be closer to them. They had lost their sister and were realizing it would be a lifetime of only being able to remember her. They were happy to return with a great experience under their belts, getting to know the family and seeing the Kiwi lifestyle. We soon found a house to rent on the same street where we had lived before leaving Seattle.

Within a week, I was fortunate to be given a job to help manage the restoration of a trawler called the *Green Hope* that initially came to Kodiak in 1983 with three other boats built by our sister company in Alabama. The *Green Hope* also fished for our Kodiak company until 2001, when it was put out of service and towed to Seattle.

It needed extensive work and a complete overhaul and preparations for the restoration began. Unfortunately, this project was abandoned after about four months due to finances. It had to wait until 2014 to be finally overhauled and now fishes in the Bering Sea and the Aleutian Islands, fishing with the company's factory trawlers fleet.

I still wanted to be connected to the church fish business and offered my services to the factory trawler fishing company that fished in Alaska. At that time it was a small company and there wasn't a position for me.

Ruptured Achilles tendon

I didn't have the heart to go back to a sales position and decided to work for myself as a contractor.

Buying a van and tools was the first step to starting my plumbing and construction business. When I was thirteen, I had joined the local tennis club and have always enjoyed the game. It is a great game, even for elderly folks. Unfortunately, over the years, I seldom played. When my son asked me to play tennis on a Saturday afternoon. I jumped at the chance to spend time with him.

Not long into the game, I suddenly felt like someone had hit me with a two-by-four in the back of my right leg below the calf and I spun around, ready to defend myself, finding no one there. Then the pain set in and I realized I couldn't walk. I knew I was in trouble. I had most likely torn a muscle of some kind.

At the hospital, without insurance, I was told that I had torn my Achilles tendon. I could have an operation to repair it, or they could mold a cast boot to fit, which was cheaper and would have about the same healing time as after an operation. I chose the boot and wore it for two months. So the plan to work for myself was put on hold because recovery would take nine months before the leg would be strong enough to work as a contractor.

Life had struck some heavy blows and, using boxing terminology, I was on the ropes. After months without income money was running low, with only enough to get us through a few more months. I had misjudged how long it would take for my leg to heal and get back to work.

I had rented a house and had three teenagers to take care of and support my wife, who was waiting in New Zealand to obtain a permanent visa. The children received their New Zealand passports before we left the U.S., but Izabela could not become a New Zealand citizen.

That experience helped me to have compassion for those less fortunate than myself. Medical expenses and ill health can be devastating to one's financial situation. I know some lazy people don't want to work, but many others find life too difficult for many reasons and just give up. Many situations in a person's life can find them in hard times. I only had two choices and decided to do the best I could.

I was down to my last rental payment without help when God intervened.

My good friend Andrew, who knew I was unemployed, called me and said he could get me a job with Matthy, who we both knew. I had first met him when he visited Kodiak years before to buy salmon.

I felt the hand of God as I went to work each day. The strangest thing was there was little for me to do. The office was at the water's edge with a stunning view of Seattle. The office was originally a house that had been converted and marble flooring and walls were still the main decor.

Only the owner, a secretary and I worked there. I asked the boss what he expected me to do and he said to go through his financials for the last few years and look at sales, etc. I still didn't have much to do and a few days later, I gave him a list of possible projects and asked him which would help him.

He traveled to Europe often and I found out later that he was trying to sell his company to a European company. I initially thought that he hired me to show those looking to buy the company that he had someone with experience, as I had managed a company in Alaska and had seven years of sales experience in Seattle. After a short time, I realized he genuinely wanted to help me.

Either way, I felt the hand of God. It isn't until you get into callous times that you can recognize the help of God when it comes.

After nearly two months, I told my boss I couldn't take his money without doing something more constructive to pay my way. He was a well-organized, savvy businessman. Everything he touched was immaculately done, all the ingredients for success.

But he didn't need me, so I handed in my notice. He was very kind and gracious and we parted on good terms.

God works in a person's life through other good people. Over the years, I have tried to be more sensitive, listening to others for a message from heaven being relayed to me.

I was having second thoughts about starting my own business. It had been thirty-two years since I worked as a plumber in New Zealand and I needed more experience to work as a plumber or heating installer in America.

A company advertising for help hired me and they paid me a lower wage based on my lack of experience. I couldn't cover all the monthly bills and asked for a raise after a month, but was declined.

I had decided to leave if I wasn't given a raise in pay, so I found myself without a job again. Often, when things don't work out how you hoped, something else actually turns out to be the best outcome.

Looking through Craigslist job offerings, I noticed a job offer for a geothermal installer, which I wanted to learn about. I was hired to install the mechanical piping for their installs. I discovered the company was in financial distress.

Being the last to be hired, I was laid off within three months.

My plumbing and heating business

2008, was the start of the economic hard times for the country – not the best time to start my own company.

I was a little "long in the tooth" to start my own plumbing and construction business at fifty-seven. I didn't have the finances or the experience to hire someone to help me and I wondered if I could work and operate my own business. I quickly found it very hard to work on my own every day.

It was a far cry from managing the Kodiak processing company, employing over 250 people with two shifts. I had no contacts initially and put my name on Craigslist looking for work.

At my first job, the lady complained and I didn't get paid. It was not the best start for the new venture, but over the next eleven years, that only happened once again when an owner only paid me for half the contract because he had run out of funds.

Adrian, whom I became friends with while working at the geothermal company for eight years, was from Romania and the best tradesman I had ever worked with.

He was intelligent and kind to everyone and was a dedicated Christian with a wonderful family. He was always gracious if I called and asked him questions about the different plumbing and heating systems. He knew I was trained in plumbing but never understood how different plumbing was in New Zealand. The American plumbing codes and systems differed from when I was plumbing in New Zealand.

Everything was new and I had to learn about plumbing, heating systems and air conditioning quickly.

I quickly learned that working in construction, plumbing, heating and air conditioning was complex. It is very physical, complicated to install without problems and always challenging to master and with the changing technology, there are always new products to know about.

Working out of a van and ensuring I was carrying all the tools and equipment for a project was a constant concern. It was very stressful to work for contractors and homeowners who required the very best and it was always challenging to ensure I ran a good business and completed every job without mistakes.

Heart attack

It was the end of May 2015 when I woke up early in the morning with sweat on my neck and felt generally unwell. I had planned a busy day and thought I would go back to sleep for a while and hopefully feel better after a nap.

I pulled the blankets over my head, but a small voice said, That's not a good idea. Something is wrong and you better take care of it.

There were no prior indications that I had any problems leading up to this event. Blood lab work showed everything was normal and I rarely needed to go to a doctor, but something felt off. I woke my wife and told her I wasn't feeling well and asked her to drive me to the hospital. I was starting to feel worse as we got to the hospital.

I walked in, telling them I was feeling bad and they laid me on a gurney and wheeled me into surgery to have two stents immediately installed in my arteries.

I could have died if I hadn't listened to that small voice telling me to get out of bed. I had another chance to change and perfect myself.

Maybe the stress of life had caught up to me. I had always been very interested in health and this setback pushed me to research more about natural health. Doctors can generally find out what is weak in the body, but I feel it is up to the individual to maintain their health. My philosophy is the body will heal itself if given the right conditions.

After eleven years, I was forced to retire due to Covid restrictions in 2019. My wife and I decided not to take the vaccine and instead built up our immunity with supplements. We did get COVID eventually and didn't suffer any serious health issues.

Helicopter crash

Father Moon mentioned after the helicopter crash in 2008, his daily exercises strengthened his body, saving him from serious injury.

He was eighty-eight years old and Mother Moon was sixty-five when they crashed into the side of a mountain at Chung Pyung, South Korea.

The helicopter pilot had lost visibility due to heavy fog on the approach to the landing pad. It was indeed a miracle that the sixteen people on board survived because the helicopter exploded after they escaped the wreckage. There were no serious injuries, but a young woman received a minor spinal injury during the crash.

That day, many miracles protected them. The tail of the helicopter got caught in a Y-shaped tree as it crashed, preventing the helicopter from spinning on the ground, where it would have exploded sooner.

Freedom

The search for freedom has been a big motivator in my life. I quickly notice a war within myself if I feel trapped by life. I have made drastic changes and decisions when I felt stuck or things weren't right.

I read comments from people who mention feeling enslaved and trapped by a religious lifestyle, but I have never felt that way. I am grateful to have met the Unificationist Movement. Because of this, I think my life became more meaningful, creating a family and supporting Father and Mother Moon's vision even in the small way I helped. I do feel that I haven't done enough.

I sometimes question my belief about understanding the Messiah because having so many opportunities to work closely with Father and Mother Moon made it easy to look at them as ordinary people.

It is a vast concept to think the Messiah is on earth. Recognizing the Lord of the Second Advent coming on the clouds would be much easier. Through my intimate experiences with them in Kodiak, I believe my faith was strengthened because I saw how they lived and breathed a life dedicated to God.

I'll never forget how they sacrificed everything to create a world of peace, beauty and goodness.

Forgiving the Enemy

The foundation of Christianity is rooted in Forgiveness. It began with Jesus, who forgave those who crucified him. When we look at the pitiful situation of Jesus's death, he was virtually alone with only a few disciples, his mother, Mary and two thieves on each side. The situation looked hopeless. How could anything good come from such a miserable death?

This is the greatness of love. Jesus overcame and conquered all by forgiving those who killed him. The religious leaders, the Sanhedrin of Judges, had decided on his fate with a vote for or against his crucifixion. Some voted no, but the majority voted yes.

Jesus came with a new message of love, proclaiming God sent him, but he didn't meet their concepts of who the Messiah should be. They were waiting for a king from the lineage of David to overthrow Roman rule. When Jesus appeared, humble without formal education, fame, or fortune, it was too challenging for them to believe in him.

They were caught up in rituals and traditions and wouldn't listen to his new teachings. Father Moon told one fellow prisoner that no matter what dogma you follow or what particular faith you have, if you don't have love, God's love for humanity, people and the creation, then the law doesn't mean much.

God's love is greater than God's law.

Forgiveness is a mighty force and through it, Jesus was able to change humanity.

Father Moon always stressed loving your enemy in all situations in life. He was the most remarkable example of showing us how to love and forgive the enemy. Even our wives, husbands, children, family members and friends would sometimes become our enemies. We have to forgive them, sometimes many times in our lives. We have to forgive ourselves and the enemy within. Forgiveness is no longer a theory. Now, we have to decide how to act.

Striking first is the tactic of evil. God's heart is to forgive and melt the heart of anger and resentment by forgiving, loving and serving others. Forgiveness is such a powerful weapon that it melts and disintegrates the hatred of the offender.

Eugene, the feeling of wanting to forgive you definitely came from somewhere beyond and surprised me. Knowing Jin Joo's character, we knew she would be the first to forgive you and we believe she did forgive you first. We were determined to defy the evil force that had used you by forgiving you. All we could do was remember the principle of forgiveness and how it always claims victory for good.

I thought, *How would our Teacher Moon act in this situation?* He was the example we always wanted to follow, but this path was uncharted. He would surely take the way of forgiveness.

We had read many stories about how he had forgiven the Japanese guards who had tortured him to near death when they imprisoned him for participating in the Korean independence movement as a student in Japan.

When the Second World War ended in August 1945, Father Moon persuaded fellow Koreans not to take revenge on the local Japanese officials. They would have been executed if he had not helped to get them safe transport back to Japan.

Take down the cross

In December of 2003, I accompanied Christian ministers on a Middle East Peace Pilgrimage with over two hundred Ambassadors for Peace in the Holy Land.

This was one of the earliest of more than forty pilgrimages organized over a few years to bring religious and political leaders to Israel to help build peace between the three Abrahamic faiths: Judaism, Christianity and Islam.

During our visit to Jerusalem and its vicinity, we encountered the beginnings of Christianity. We retraced Jesus Christ's footsteps to Golgotha, where he was tragically crucified.

It was inspiring to see thousands of Israelis and Palestinians join us as we marched through Jerusalem, shouting for Peace. Shalom. Salam aleykum.

I experienced very profound feelings and emotions during that week. We visited many sacred sites. The most memorable was the Mount of Olives, where Jesus prayed earnestly before being taken before Pontius Pilate.

I thought about Jesus' three closest disciples, Peter, James and John. They couldn't understand the seriousness of the situation and fell asleep rather than praying with Jesus.

Judaism, Islam and Christianity are sharply divided against each other in today's world, even though they share a common root. The issue that keeps them divided is their understanding of Jesus.

In 2001, Father Moon asked all Christian Ministers and Pastors to remove the crosses from their churches, a shocking request even for our members because this symbolized Christianity and we knew it would be a tough pill for Christians to swallow.

Members contacted ministers to relay Father's message and a few churches proceeded to take down their crosses, but this was an impossible request for most. We know one church in Seattle that does not display a Cross but a Dove representing the Holy Spirit.

He said we should take down the crosses to heal and unite the religions. To Muslims, Jews, Buddhists and many others, the cross symbolizes intolerance, prejudice and dominionism, not love and forgiveness. It is a pagan symbol, the Roman instrument for capital punishment. Most importantly, it is a remembrance of a great tragedy for humanity. However, to many Christians, it is a symbol of Jesus' victory, requesting to take down the cross is an impossible hurdle to overcome.

The cross was specifically significant to Jews who have been persecuted throughout history. Islam, on the other hand, teaches that Jesus never died on the cross. Displaying the symbol of the cross can be another dividing issue.

Following Jesus' words, Father Moon said that Christians now should carry the cross in their hearts and de-emphasize displaying the cross in their relations with other Abrahamic faiths.

Eugene, without true reconciliation, our families or nations will not achieve true peace. Reconciliation always encompasses forgiveness, compassion and a will to apologize, repent, leave behind the past and focus on building a better future.

The main message of Dr. Martin Luther King is to love your enemies. Maybe we can say something more. Religious leaders must lead the way in loving and reconciling historical enemies.

I gave up my seat to a Christian minister on the bus that would take us to meet with the late Yasser Arafat, the President of the state of Palestine at the time. I was sorry to have missed that historic meeting, but it was more important for a Christian Minister to attend than I.

At Al Aqsa Mosque, where the marchers were welcomed and held a prayer meeting before continuing on to the Western Wall.

Crowds of pilgrims gathered around the Al Aqsa Mosque.

Every religion should contribute to world peace because there is nothing more fearful than a religious war, as both sides never give up and are ready to die for their beliefs.

Father Moon brought together forty religious scholars to compare the sacred teachings of Judaism, Christianity, Islam, Buddhism and other major world religions. They found that the sacred texts of many religions convey the same or very similar messages more than seventy percent of the time, showing that the teachings are the same at their core.

God's way is always the way of harmony, seeking reconciliation and peace.

Father Moon's passing

Father Moon died from pneumonia-related complications in Korea on September 3, 2012, at ninety-two years of age.

He was being treated in the hospital and told everyone that he couldn't stay in the hospital because there was much more to do. He insisted on being discharged. Reluctantly, they agreed.

He had worked tirelessly even into advanced age and made frequent speaking tours abroad. In the last year of his life, he crossed the Pacific Ocean eight times. His schedule was always strict, rising at 3:00 a.m. to pray, exercise and study. This took a heavy toll on his body and caused respiratory disease.

He felt responsible for healing the broken world and pushed himself beyond his limits. His life of dedication, hardships and difficulties would have taken a younger man earlier, but he was born with incredible health and vitality, living to an old age.

Still, it was a challenging time for the Movement when he passed. We felt lost. He had given everything to train us and show us how to resemble God's heart with a desire to save each human being.

Some news outlets commented that the prospects for the church looked bleak as the founder had passed. Could the next generation take up the mantle, a crucial test for a new religion?

Little did we understand that Mother Moon, who had been by his side and co-led the movement for fifty-two years, would lead the movement from that point on.

I read both of their autobiographies and the section that moved my heart in the *Mother of Peace* book is where she tells the story of how Father Moon asked her to sit facing him during breakfast the day before he died. It was customary for them to sit side by side during meals, but he wasn't interested in eating. As she explained in the book, he gazed at her to engrave her face in his heart.

They loved and respected each other and we witnessed how they enjoyed each other's company and had many happy times together in Kodiak.

After his passing, Mother Moon offered three years of devotion, visiting his grave every day, rain or shine, which is an old Korean tradition to be fulfilled by the eldest son or a spouse.

God prepares through difficulties and sacrifice

Eugene, God has always prepared special people in history through hardship and pain. How else could they learn to endure and continue to go to the victorious end? Like the process of steel going into fire and being tempered, coming out harder and sharper.

My heart grieves as I study the life of Father Moon. The years of difficulty and persecution he endured throughout his life didn't prevent him from moving forward. All the powers of darkness tried to crush him. Only through the love and mercy of God was he able to achieve so much in his lifetime, more than any other man in history.

He had never prayed out of weakness but always tried to comfort God's heart. He was truly God's beloved champion, giving his life of blood, sweat and tears for humanity and heaven.

He used to say, "The dawn of a new age is slowly approaching."

The world didn't accept him on a larger scale than I had imagined when I first heard his teachings. I naively thought the religious world would come to understand these new revelations before he died.

It was difficult for the people of America to accept a man from Asia who came with a new message of God's warning to the world.

Unfortunately, history has always scorned the prophets who came to tell us that we must change. Jesus also came with new truths, showing a different understanding of God's heart. The prominent religious leaders scoffed at him, knowing he wasn't a Rabbi who had studied the Torah nor came from a prominent family and refused to recognize the one they had waited for. The elites entrenched in their biblical laws could only accept someone who came with their message.

'The Crown of Glory,' a poem by young Sun Myung Moon Expresses God's and Humanity's situation

When I doubt people, I feel pain.

When I judge people, it is unbearable.

When I hate people, there is no value

To my existence.

Yet, if I believe, I am deceived; if I love, I am betrayed.

Suffering and grieving tonight,

My head in my hands.
Am I wrong? Yes, I am wrong.
Even though we are deceived,
Still believe, though we are betrayed
Still forgive.
Love completely, even those who hate you.
Wipe your tears away and welcome with
A smile those who know nothing but
Deceit and those who betray without regret.
O master, the pain of loving,
Look at my hands, place your hand
On my chest. My heart is burning
Such agony. But when I love those
Who acted against me,
I brought victory.
If you have done the same thing,
I will give you the crown of glory.

Father Moon's life

Father Moon wasn't a Pope who was voted into his position or a priest who took over a parish. His mission started when he accepted Jesus' calling at fifteen.

He finished writing the original Divine Principle fifteen years later and started evangelizing from his first church – a mud hut made with cardboard ration boxes before the end of the Korean War.

His life must be the most remarkable story. How he was liberated from the Hungnam labor camp by UN forces after nearly three years of hard labor and then went on to build a worldwide movement during his lifetime is astounding. His unrelenting dedication to ending God's and humanity's suffering by building world peace and fulfilling the mission that Jesus asked of him will be understood in time.

Father Moon was born as the fifth son of a family of thirteen children on January 6th, 1920, in what is now North Korea. His family converted from Buddhism to Christianity when he was ten years old. In a very short time, he became a Sunday School helper, teaching children about Jesus and telling them Bible stories.

On the other hand, Mother Moon was born twenty-three years later as the only daughter of a Christian family. She was born on the same day as Father Moon, in a small town very close to Father Moon's hometown.

Japan had annexed Korea in 1910 and considered it a part of Japan. During their occupation, Japan waged war on Korean culture, religion and traditions. Christians were persecuted and forced to convert to Shintoism. Schools and universities forbade speaking Korean and emphasized loyalty to the Japanese Emperor. They were forbidden to wear white, as was customary for thousands of years in their culture, symbolizing purity, cleanliness and humility.

Spiritual groups taught that Koreans were chosen for a special purpose in God's plan for humanity and their white dress symbolized their faith that they were children of the divine light.

Oppressed Korean Christians prayed for the long-awaited Messiah, similar to the Jewish people who awaited the Messiah to deliver them from the Roman occupation. Some with unique spiritual gifts predicted that Christ would be born in their land of Korea. Koreans didn't submit easily to Japanese rule and protest movements pushed for Korean independence throughout nearly forty years of the occupation.

When Father Moon was sixteen, he went to Mount Myodu on Easter weekend to pray all night. On Easter Sunday morning, the spirit of Jesus appeared to him and asked him to continue his work of world salvation to end the suffering of humanity.

For the next nine years, he devoted himself to religious study and prayer to prepare himself to accomplish his given mission.

He traveled to Japan to study electrical engineering. He was active in the underground Korean independence movement, which resulted in the Japanese authorities taking him into custody many times and torturing him for information.

When America defeated Japan in 1945, Korea was liberated from Japanese rule, but it was divided between the North, controlled by the Soviet Union and the South, under the control of the USA.

In 1946, there was a lot of turbulence as communists took control of North Korea and Soviet troops imposed a Communist regime. The Communists started to attack organized religion and people started fleeing to the South and became refugees in their own country.

Father Moon suddenly decided to cross the border and go North to Pyongyang, a city that once had many churches and was called the Jerusalem of the East, to teach the new revelations he received from God and confront the Godless ideology of communism.

After a few months of evangelizing, he was arrested by North Korean authorities and falsely accused of being a spy sent by Syngman Rhee, the first president of South Korea. After three months of interrogations and torture, his lifeless body was thrown outside the prison walls.

Some of his early followers found him and, with herbal medicine, nursed him back to health. Soon after, he started to evangelize again. As more and more Christians began leaving their traditional churches, their ministers complained to the communist authorities about the dangers of Father Moon's activities.

In February 1948, he was taken into custody again for advocating social chaos and five months later, after severe beatings and interrogations, he was sentenced to five years in Hungnam concentration camp, the most brutal forced labor prison in North Korea, where the life expectancy for a prisoner was no longer than six months.

Around the same time in the fall of 1948, Mother Moon was five years old when her mother and grandmother left their hometown in North Korea and started their journey towards the 38th Parallel, reaching Seoul, with the help of her uncle, in June of 1950.

After reading about Father Moon's miserable situation, I am still amazed that he survived. The prisoners were forced to work hard labor, filling bags of ammonium sulfate fertilizer made from sulfuric acid, which scarred their skin. The bitter winter's cold was brutal while sustaining on little more than a bowl of weak seaweed salty soup and a few hard rice balls per day.

As UN forces were approaching Hungnam, his life was in jeopardy as the guards systematically executed the prisoners. The UN forces bombed Hungnam and liberated the rest of the prisoners. He was finally free after enduring two years and eight months of hell on earth. God had indeed protected him through this unbearable time.

Immediately, Father Moon decided to get to Pyongyang to find his early followers. Unfortunately, after searching for forty days, he found only a few. One of them was a man with a broken leg who had been discharged from Hungnam labor camp earlier. The other was a young eighteen-year-old man who was a nephew of an early PyongYang member.

Teacher Moon insisted on carrying the injured man towards the Southern border. Three of them joined the line of seven miles of refugees. They pushed the man on a bike or carried him on their shoulders.

It was dangerous to carry someone as it slowed them down, but he wouldn't leave him behind, believing that this disabled man represented humankind. Even in his pitiful physical condition, he determined that he couldn't save the world if he didn't carry this person to safety.

Soon after they crossed the frozen Imjin River, the UN forces closed that crossing to any more refugees. When they finally arrived at the point where the 38th Parallel divided the peninsula, Father Moon placed one foot in South Korea and the other in North Korea and promised to God in his prayer that one day he would gather the forces of the free world to liberate North Korea and unite North and South.

After a long journey, just two of them arrived in Pusan in the cold winter of 1951.

These were difficult times as starvation plagued the land and the war decimated the infrastructure. Father Moon and his disciple Won

Pil Kim were so impoverished that they begged for food in their torn and tattered clothing.

Father wrote in his memoir, *As a Peace-Loving Global Citizen*, "Almost nothing was left of the soles of my shoes, although the upper part was mostly there. I might as well have been walking barefoot. The fact was simply that I was the lowest of the low, a beggar amongst beggars."

Father Moon initially worked nights at Pusan Harbor, which helped them rent a small room where he started to write down the first draft of the original text of the Divine Principle. Won Pil soon got a job at the UN military base painting portraits of American soldiers' wives and girlfriends from the photos they provided. He made enough money to buy rice to survive and keep Father Moon supplied with pencils.

They soon started to build a shack on a hill near the cemetery, using rocks, mud and ration boxes to make a roof. It was a small space where a small table and easel could hardly fit. That was the humble place where the first draft of the Original Divine Principle was completed.

After finishing writing, he was ready to share his teaching. Close by was a well where people used to come and the rumor started about this "handsome, crazy man" teaching a new understanding of the Bible.

One of the first women who started to listen was an evangelist, Ms. Kang, from a nearby Christian church.

After a few days of debates, she agreed to Father Moon's explanations of the Bible and became his first follower in South Korea.

The shack and a young Father Moon

In 1954, as the congregation grew, they purchased a house in Seoul and hung a sign that read Holy Spirit Association for the Unification Of World Christianity – a movement he hoped would unite all Christian denominations.

Father Moon's most profound message is that God is a grieving God in absolute misery, having seen humankind's tragic and sad history.

His early disciples have testified about how Father Moon's tearful prayers had drenched his clothes and even the floor.

Unfortunately, they were persecuted by the established churches for teaching a controversial new understanding of the Bible. He was accused of being a heretic and that his Movement was a pseudo-church. In America, he was accused of brainwashing converts and as the saying goes, if you repeat a lie enough times, people will believe it. This is what happened to Father Moon throughout the years.

His teachings attracted followers from a prominent Christian women's university, Ewha University, a school closely linked with the Korean government and mainline Protestant denominations. The University sent professors to investigate why many students were joining Father Moon's church.

When some of the professors also joined, more persecution followed and the University president ordered the professors and students to either stop going to the Moon's church or be expelled. They chose to leave the school and continue attending their new church.

Established churches began their persecution of this new religious movement. Seoul newspapers began to print alarming stories about the Unification Church, calling it a promiscuous group and saying that Moon was a North Korean agent. He was soon thrown in jail and released weeks later when no charges could be found.

The following year, he was again imprisoned on charges of evading the military draft, even though he had been an inmate in Hungnam prison during the time in question. When he was sent to jail, there was so much sensational media coverage, but when he was released after several months when the charges were dropped, his release received very little notice in the press.

Foremost, his persecution came from religious leaders, the government and the media to suppress this new movement and Father Moon's activities. His growing membership would attract more and more persecution. That would become the pattern for his ministry throughout his whole life.

Amidst this tribulation, Father Moon nurtured an ever-growing community of early faithful disciples in Korea, primarily women who thought he exaggerated when he spoke to them about the future and that a worldwide movement centering on America would soon stem from their small group.

By 1957, his missionaries had established thirty churches in Korean cities and towns. In 1958, the first missionary went to Japan. Then, in 1959, the first missionaries came to America.

Ministry in America

In 1971, Father Moon fulfilled the vision he had spoken of to his early disciples when he came to America to expand his ministry worldwide.

The United States was a country that God had so richly blessed, embracing people of all races and religions – representing the world. What happens in America certainly does have global repercussions.

Mother of Peace continues

Mother Moon's mother became a very dedicated follower of Father Moon and introduced her daughter, Hak Ja Han, to him. Father and Mother Moon were Blessed in Marriage in 1960. They had fourteen children and she would accompany Father Moon to every public event until his passing in 2012.

For years before he passed, she gave speeches in many countries on behalf of Father Moon. He would watch her speeches that were broadcast live. They spent over fifty years together and she, the Mother of Peace, continued to fulfill her pledge to her husband to realize their shared world peace dreams, starting with unifying North and South Korea.

During their lives together, they accomplished much in a relatively short period. They worked tirelessly to realize a world of peace. This was not only confined to religion but endeavors that would bring beauty and goodness to the world through education, philosophy, science, religion, media, arts, technology, charitable works, the environment, families, women, and youth – all based on an ideal of true love. All these efforts took tremendous amounts of church funds and resources to accomplish God's ideal.

I was very fortunate to spend some time with them in Kodiak, Alaska, to see their life's commitment to planting seeds for a future world of peace.

As their youngest son, Hyung Jin Moon, said, "There is no religious founder who has accomplished this much in his or her lifetime and the foundation extends worldwide."

No saint or prophet has ever been welcomed in his historical age. Only a hundred or a thousand years after their death, when his bones have changed to dust, does he become a historic object of reverence.

That has been the path of saints so far in history. History has always scorned the prophets who came to tell us that we must change. God always brings a new message at different times according to our level of maturity.

In the near future, many more people will study Father Moon's teachings and realize that the Messiah and His Bride, God's only begotten daughter, fulfilled the prophecy of the Marriage Supper of the Lamb and began building the kingdom of God on this earth.

Memorial Bench in Charlotte's Park

In 2007, Mothers of Murdered Offspring (MoMO) held a memorial service at Frazier Park near downtown Charlotte, North Carolina. We attended this event in the beautiful garden where Jin Joo's memorial plaque was placed.

Children's Memorial Walkway in the Frazer Park in Charlotte, North Carolina.

A few months later, we asked our friends to help us purchase a cast iron bench, now installed in the children's memorial park. The "Bench of Love and Forgiveness" was dedicated in her honor and is a permanent memorial of a very personal nature for Jin Joo. It waits for those who wish to rest and contemplate.

Eugene, I hope you can visit one day, sit on her bench, and say a prayer.

Please remember the Children's Memorial Walkway, made of engraved bricks, laid carefully side by side, each bears the name of a loved child.

You will walk on holy ground because each brick represents terrible loss, pain, and devastation.

Continuation of Personal Letter

Eugene,

It has been twenty-one years since we lost our eldest precious daughter.

Jin Joo Ellen was an extraordinary young woman at the age of eighteen, as you can see from the many testimonials about her good and unique personality. Of course, we had something to do with the molding of her character. Still, the essential influence was that she grew up surrounded by a community of men and women of faith, those who searched for and exemplified goodness, those who sacrificed their lives for something far greater than themselves.

In our life journey, we are fortunate to find even one person who will show us a heart of goodness and love. We will never forget that person. True goodness is so rare, like a magnet: it will pull and draw in those who seek such things.

It is not only our family that still grieves for her, but the whole community who knew and loved her grieved not only for her but for the ideal and hope she represented.

My heart goes to those who have lost their loved ones, especially a child. Words are not enough to convey the sense of loss a parent bears. It is a terrible calamity to be left only with a photo of your loved one propped up on the mantelpiece. I have seen how my children have suffered losing their elder sister, who should have been there at all the special events in their lives to celebrate their birthdays, school and college graduations, welcome their children into the world and be Aunty Jin Joo Ellen.

Generations of laughter and hope for the future have been silenced. I have thought long and hard, wondering how to convey to you the thoughts, the pain and the emotions of a father and a man striving for holiness in his lifetime. How does a man treat someone who has murdered his daughter?

We will never forget our daughter of goodness and beauty, who died far too young. The death of Jin Joo Ellen has broken our hearts and our family and her friends have suffered greatly. My wife and I were on a roller coaster of emotions, feeling great sorrow, emptiness and pain even though we had three other children.

We had been trained in spiritual life and had felt and seen the presence of the spiritual reality, but it was still so hard to feel total comfort that she was okay. We wondered where she was in the spiritual realm, inhabiting a world of love, but here, she was gone forever and we couldn't do anything about it.

We thought we would have many more years with her and were looking forward to seeing her with a husband and children but now, tragically, that wasn't going to be. I wanted to relive and cherish those times together and regretted not spending more precious moments. My heart grieves for any parent who regrets not giving enough.

Life caught up to me and I stopped writing. I lost confidence in my ability to write and convey thoughts and emotions. I wasn't able to start again for years. I think it was too painful. When I did begin again, the writings I had saved on a floppy disc had become corrupted and I had to start again. Written words aren't sufficient to express my heart. There were days of deep sadness when it was too painful and I could type only a few lines before doing something else to escape. We need to treat each other with more compassion, as many people go about their lives with great pain and sad life stories.

A person can damage their life and future instantly. Unfortunately, this is the step you have taken. We all live in very turbulent times because the world has reached a crossroads as a new culture of the heart will blossom for the world to see. The waves of change are now touching the world, so I wanted to share about our lives and how God has guided us in our journey.

I have always been a searcher, looking for the truth in everything. I seek an ideal world that seems lost and impossible to realize. Because Jin Joo Ellen died so young, in such a tragic way, my idealism was lost for a time. It has been a long process to get it back. I now wonder if humanity can ever create and live in a world of true beauty, free of hate and injustice. People have such diverse beliefs. I wonder if we can finally make a world of peace and unity or if we are destined to eventually separate into areas of the world with those who have similar beliefs. I believe the ideal does lie deep in every person's heart and soul but easily gets clouded over in the process of life and exposure to all that is false.

Every parent fears that they could lose their child to a sickness, accident, war, street or school shooting, God forbid. It is a topic that isn't easily discussed because what you talk about sometimes does come true. In the quiet of the night, they wonder how they could ever deal with the death of their child. Death does bring commonality to humanity because we all grieve for our loved ones. Our tears flow the same.

We thank you for your letters and the cards from your mother. They are painful to read because we can only imagine how difficult it is for you to fulfill a forty-year jail sentence. I'm not sure if you realize that you would have received the death penalty if we hadn't pleaded for your life.

One of the most important reasons was we wanted you to have time to redeem yourself and realize what you have done and how it affected you, your family and us. Unfortunately, you will spend the best years of your life in jail.

I have often thought about why we must forgive you, as it seems unbelievable to most people. The primary motivation was defiance of the evil that used you to murder our precious daughter. Through this devastating experience, we saw more clearly a sad world and couldn't bear to witness one more death or another life lost, another insult to the beauty of life: one more weeping parent or another lost soul. We needed to do one decent act in a world that seems lost.

Eugene, I had listened to sermons through the years that forgiveness wasn't only for the forgiven but more for the forgiver to free their soul of all that would destroy them. It would not be an immediate feeling, but eventually, with time, healing would happen. Our lives would never be the same. We had to carry on and live a life that Jin Joo would be proud of and forgiveness would be the first step.

Eugene, we forgive you because we know God wants to forgive you. To be free of hate and vengeance is the only way we can continue our lives now and we believe that our forgiveness also frees Jin Joo Ellen in the spiritual realm from resentment and disappointment from losing her physical body in such a terrible way. Our lives are very short compared to eternity and what is important and meaningful on this earth is to live a life of honesty, goodness, purity and truth.

We will not give up our belief in ultimate goodness nor hope that this world can improve, where goodness and beauty prevail. If every child is given the right opportunity and environment, then all that is good and pure will shine through that child.

That will happen if they are taught to love God and respect themselves, their parents, their family and the environment. If the child isn't given such a nurturing environment, all that seeks to destroy that innocence will succeed.

I promised that I would not allow our daughter's death to be in vain. A big part of me died with our daughter's death, but my heart has been resurrected. I have inherited more of a spiritual desire to delve even deeper into my soul, to pull out what was trapped and hidden, the original me that had the answer within me.

We have gone through periods where everything that seemed important became irrelevant. Pain and grief could turn our hearts to or away from God. Her passing has awakened our souls. Our hearts have been pried open and we can sense our soul, which is unconditional love. We can sense the fragrance of that love that can weep for the suffering of humanity and rejoice at the smallest act of kindness — standing up for what we believe now seems more important. I know the only way to survive is by serving and loving others who need help. I will always wake up every day for the rest of my life and think about Jin Joo Ellen, our first beloved daughter.

Through Jin Joo Ellen's death, we can more profoundly feel humanity's grief. Only in times of hardship and sorrow can most people sense God and connect with His suffering heart.

Because God has given us free will, He can't intervene to prevent us from doing evil. It is up to us to choose the righteous way. God is a parent and, like any parent, never wants to destroy his children. God has a father's and a mother's qualities, thus, we call him Heavenly Parent.

I empathize with God when I think of the pain and misery of life and see evil people who do well and seem to win the day through their lies and deceit. I must keep reminding myself that God's hands are tied and he can't interfere. He is waiting for us to change and become like Him, loving, forgiving, patient and persevering.

Yours Truly,

Martyn Byrne

About the Author

Martyn Byrne was born and raised in New Zealand. He traveled to the United States in 1977, searching for a truth to guide his life.

Without any previous writing experience, he completed this letter of forgiveness to the man who murdered his eldest daughter. The letter developed into a manuscript of his journey to find the ideal.

The hope for happiness through the family and faith is implicit in the story.

He retired from self-employment in construction and a long career earlier in the fish business centered in Alaska.

He lives in Seattle with his wife of forty-two years and their pampered dog. He is proud of his three remaining children and grandchildren and looks forward to seeing many more little feet.

Milton Keynes UK
Ingram Content Group UK Ltd.
UKHW020209170724
445403UK00005B/73/J